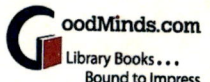

This book was purchased from
GoodMinds.com
Library Books...
Bound to Impress

To Re-Order 1.877.862.8483/www.goodminds.com

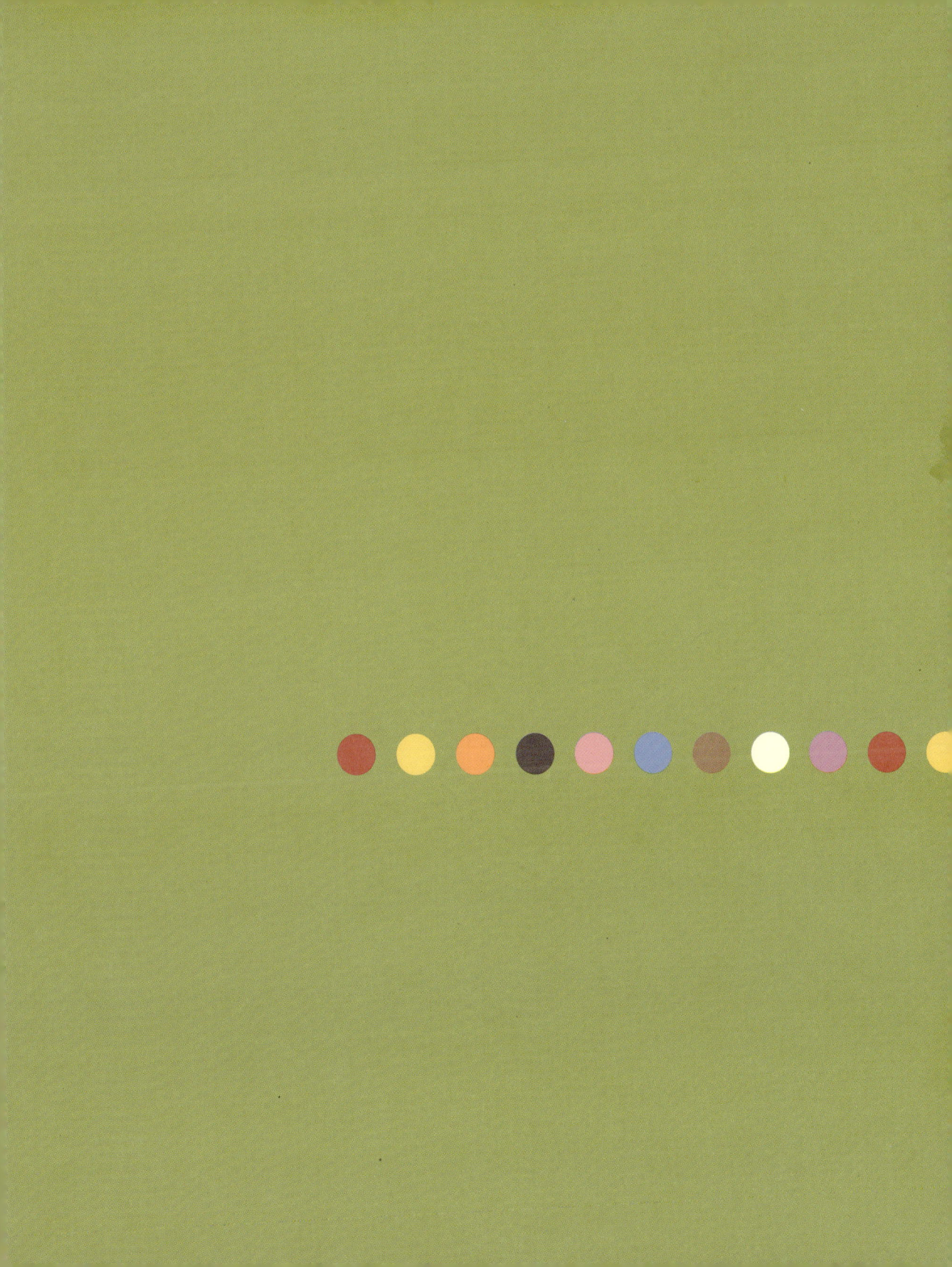

first in Canada

AN ABORIGINAL BOOK OF DAYS

Jonathan Anuik

© 2011 Canadian Plains Research Center.

All rights reserved. No part of this work covered by the copyrights hereon may be reproduced or used in any form or by any means—graphic, electronic, or mechanical—without the prior written permission of the publisher. Any request for photocopying, recording, taping or placement in information storage and retrieval systems of any sort shall be directed in writing to Access Copyright.

Printed and bound in Canada at Friesens.

The text of this book is printed on 100% post-consumer recycled paper with earth-friendly vegetable-based inks.

Cover image: "Divinity So Divine " by George Littlechild, 2004.
Acrylic and mixed media on canvas, 24" x 24" x 1.75"

Library and Archives Canada Cataloguing in Publication

Anuik, Jonathan, 1980-
First in Canada : an Aboriginal book
of days / [researched by Jonathan Anuik].

(Trade books based in scholarship, 1482-9886 ; 29)
ISBN 978-0-88977-240-3

1. Native peoples—Canada--History.
2. Native peoples—Canada—History—Calendars.
I. Title. II. Series: TBS ; 29

E78.C2A586 2011   971.004'97   C2011-906528-2

10   9   8   7   6   5   4   3   2   1

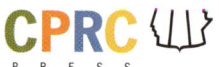

Canadian Plains Research Center Press
University of Regina
Regina, Saskatchewan, Canada, S4S 0A2
tel: (306) 585-4758   fax: (306) 585-4699
e-mail: canadian.plains@uregina.ca
web: www.cprcpress.ca

We acknowledge the financial support of the Government of Canada through the Canada Book Fund and the Saskatchewan Arts Board through the Grants to Publishers fund for our publishing activities.

 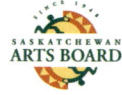

"What is life?

It is a flash of a firefly in the night.

It is a breath of a buffalo in the winter time.

It is as the little shadow that

runs across the grass and loses itself

in the sunset."

—CROWFOOT, BLACKFOOT TRIBAL CHIEF

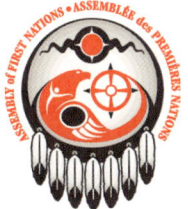

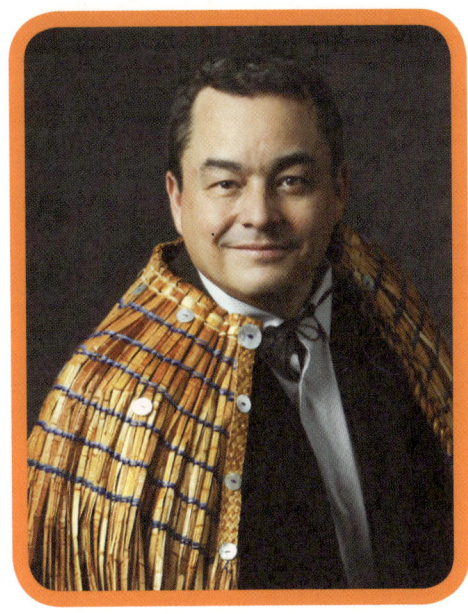

Canada is built on a proud heritage of strong, vibrant Indigenous Nations. *First in Canada* presents a look at some of the unique accomplishments of First Nation peoples and issues and events that have influenced Canadian society. In recognizing the cultural, political and economic contributions of First Nations, we have an opportunity to build a stronger Canada for all of us.

As First Nations move forward in our efforts to give life to our rights, strengthen our governments and improve the conditions for First Nation citizens and communities, we must do so in partnership and understanding with all citizens of this country. We must shake away the myths and misconceptions that block our path to progress and prosperity. Raising awareness of First Nation history and the reality of life in our communities today is fundamental to fostering real change.

First in Canada is a tremendous educational resource that reflects on the accomplishments that enrich our lives, contribute to our future and inspire us as Indigenous people. I believe that anyone reading this book will be motivated to learn more about the issues and challenges facing First Nations and the way forward to a better future for all Canadians. *Kleco, Kleco!*

Shawn A-in-chut Atleo
National Chief, Assembly of First Nations

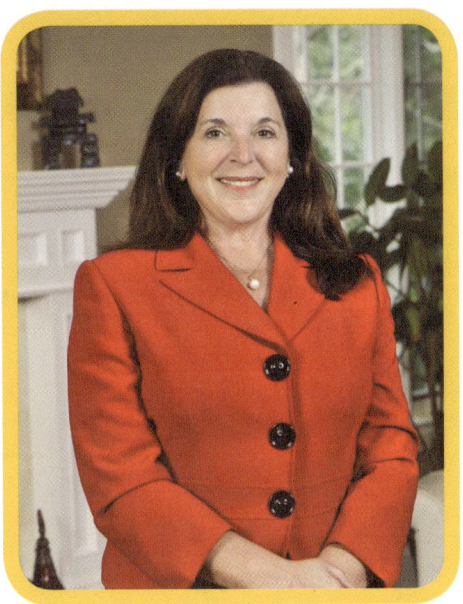

As we look to a future in which all Canadians work together to help ensure that Aboriginal peoples have the educational, political, economic and employment opportunities to achieve their rightful place in our society, it is imperative that we also look to our past. The history of Aboriginal peoples in our country—a history that is so often a source of pride, and altogether too often a source of pain—is something from which all of us must learn in order to move forward together.

By documenting the history and celebrating the cultures of our diverse First Nation, Métis and Inuit communities, *First in Canada* marks an important stage in that learning process. As a book of days, it is an ongoing celebration of past Aboriginal achievement in Canada. Perhaps more importantly, however, it stands as an inspiring reminder of the vast potential that exists in our Aboriginal communities—a potential that must be realized for the sake of all Canadians.

As you read this book, I encourage you to both reflect on our shared history and envision our shared future.

Dr. Vianne Timmons
President and Vice-Chancellor
University of Regina

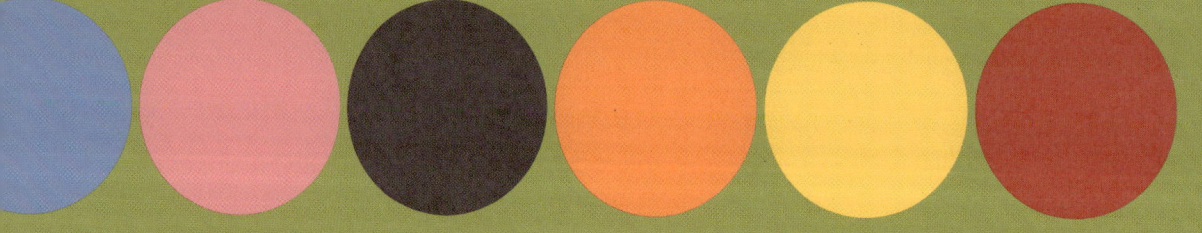

- **9000 BCE:** Aboriginal hunter-gatherers arrived on the prairies. On the northwest coast of contemporary British Columbia the ancestors of the Nisga'a, Gitksan, and Tsimshian lived in sedentary villages.

- **8600 BCE:** Scrapers to clean moose hides found in 2001 at Debert, Nova Scotia, placed the Mi'kmaq at the site at this time.

- **6000 BCE:** Hunter-gatherers such as the Assiniboine, Plains Cree, Saulteaux, and Blackfoot engaged in bison hunting.

- **c. 500 BCE–1500:** The Dorset culture thrived along the northern coastal regions of what is now Canada.

- **c. 1000 CE:** The people of the Thule culture, direct ancestors of the modern Inuit, began to spread across the Canadian Arctic, eventually displacing the previous Dorset culture.

january

stexwa7uzíken
(LILLOOET)

"Coldest Time of the Year"

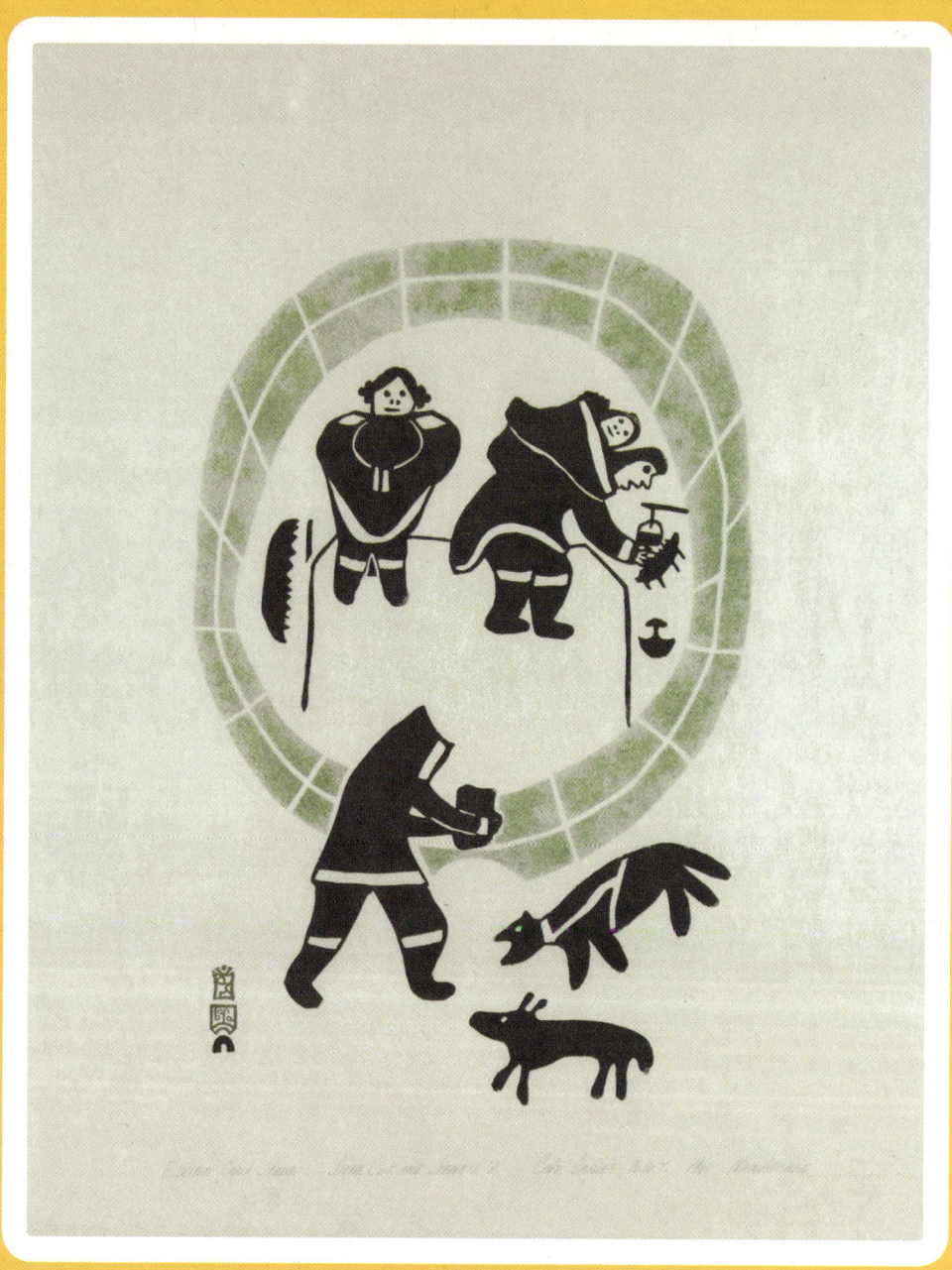

Napachie Pootoogook, *Eskimo Camp Scene.*
Stonecut and stencil on paper, 60.6 x 47.3 centimetres, 1961.

JANUARY

1 **1996.** Eddy Cobiness, an Ojibwe artist, died in Winnipeg. Born in 1933 in Minnesota, Cobiness moved to Canada and became a member of the "Indian Group of Seven."

2 **1964.** Métis leader J. Z. (Joe) LaRocque died in Lebret, Saskatchewan. ▶

1928. Saskatchewan artist Allen Sapp was born at the Red Pheasant Reserve.

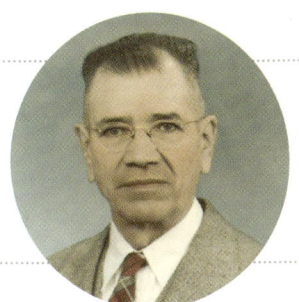

3

4 **2007.** Rt. Rev. Mark MacDonald was appointed National Indigenous Anglican Bishop of Canada. ▶

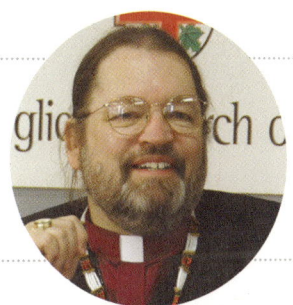

5 **2001.** Representatives of the Government of Canada and the Band government of Fishing Lake First Nation signed a draft Settlement Agreement which awarded $34.5 million for land surrendered to the federal government in 1907.

6 **1966.** *The Drum* was first published in the western Arctic.

7

The Story of the Beothuk

The discovery, treatment, and gradual extinction of the Beothuk by the Europeans who settled on their land serves as a sobering example of the attitudes adopted by those settlers towards the First Nations people living in what became Canada. At the turn of the 16th century, Portuguese explorers first encountered the Beothuk in what is now known as the province of Newfoundland and Labrador. The Beothuk spent winters on the interior of the island living off the caribou and other game of that area and moved downriver along the coast each summer to hunt seal and salmon. The arrival of settlers, however, sent them further inland, as those who stayed behind were caught and enslaved. The Beothuk covered their skin in red ochre which caused the settles to refer to them as Red Indians, a label which soon was used in reference to all the First Nations people across the continent. As European settlers continued to arrive in what would become Newfoundland and Labrador, their contact with the Beothuk increased, and the resources available to the Beothuk diminished significantly. For example, the Europeans erected weirs at the mouths of rivers in order to capture greater numbers of salmon, so the Beothuk could no longer fish for them. Any Beothuk caught raiding these weirs was killed. As contact with the Europeans often meant enslavement, if not death, the Beothuk isolated themselves inland to such a degree that the number of Beothuk dropped significantly, as many succumbed to disease when their resources dwindled. By the early 19th century, the Europeans decided to capture a Beothuk person, but now with the intention of making peace, and learning more about the culture they themselves helped decimate. Three Beothuk women, a mother and two daughters, were found and captured in 1823, all in very poor health. The mother and one of the daughters died shortly after their capture, but the remaining daughter, Shawnadithit, became employed as domestic help and saw several further attempts by the Europeans to capture more of her people. She died in 1829 and was considered the last of the Beothuk, a First Nations people who lost their land and livelihoods at the hands of explorers and settlers, who only sought to learn more about them when it was too late. (JAMES OSTIME)

JANUARY

8 — **1820.** Demasduwit (Mary March), one of the last of the Beothuks and the aunt of Shawnadithit, died at the Bay of Exploits, Newfoundland. ▶

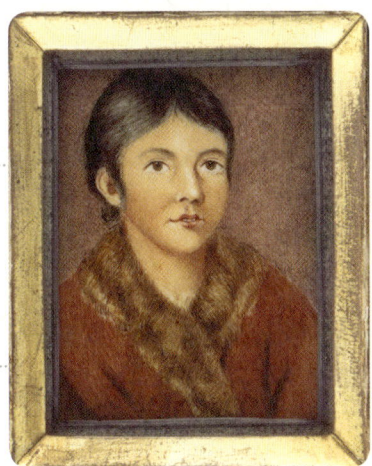

9 — **1999.** Ken Ward, Cree activist, was featured on CBC Newsworld for his work in HIV prevention and treatment.

10 — **1946.** First Nations leaders gathered at Duck Lake to decide to join with North American Indian Brotherhood.

11 — **1864.** Musquakie (William Yellowhead), Ojibwe Chief, died on the Rama Reserve, Lake Simcoe, Ontario.

12 — **1920.** Bill Reid, Haida artist, was born in Victoria, British Columbia.

13 — **1999.** "Amarok's Song: Journey to Nunavut," premiered on Vision TV; it was co-directed by Inuit Martin Kreelak and Ole Gjerstad.

14 — **1993.** Mike Cardinal, MLA, was sworn in as Alberta's first Status First Nation cabinet minister.

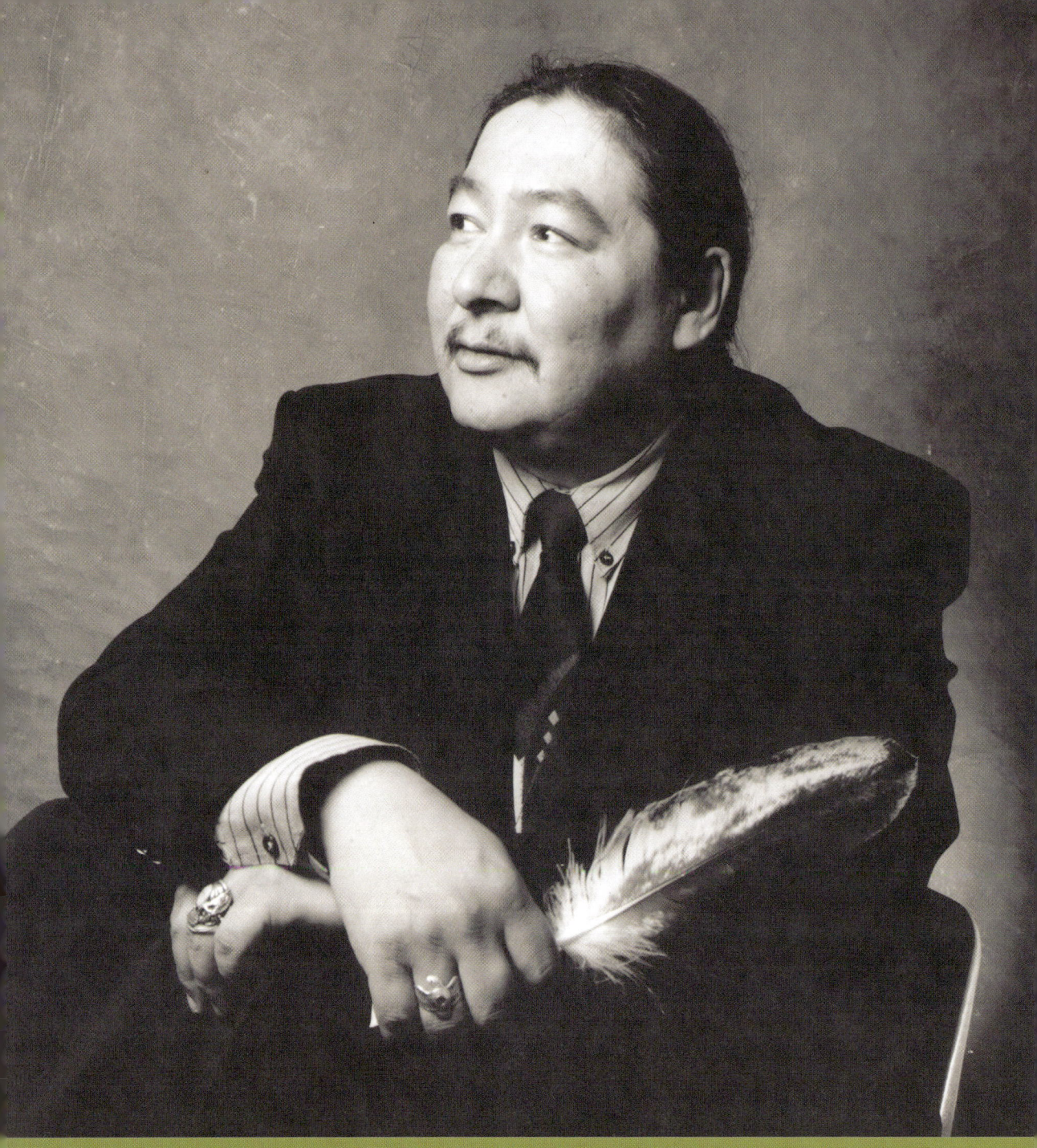

Elijah Harper.
See January 21.

JANUARY

15

16 **1991.** Assembly of First Nations Chief Leonard Tomah of Woodstock First Nation in New Brunswick delivered a presentation to the European Parliament on the challenges that face Aboriginals in Canada.

17 **1888.** Big Bear died at the Poundmaker Reserve.

18 **1983.** The stakeholders in the recently formed Métis Constitutional Alliance sent a message to Prime Minister Pierre Trudeau announcing their departure from the Native Council of Canada. The authors of the message asked that the Prime Minister recognize the Métis Constitutional Alliance as the representative for the Métis at subsequent constitutional conferences.

19 **1950.** Peter Ittinuar, the first Inuit NDP MP, was born at Chesterfield Inlet, Northwest Territories. ▶

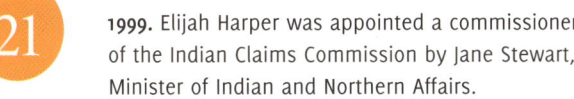

20

21 **1999.** Elijah Harper was appointed a commissioner of the Indian Claims Commission by Jane Stewart, Minister of Indian and Northern Affairs.

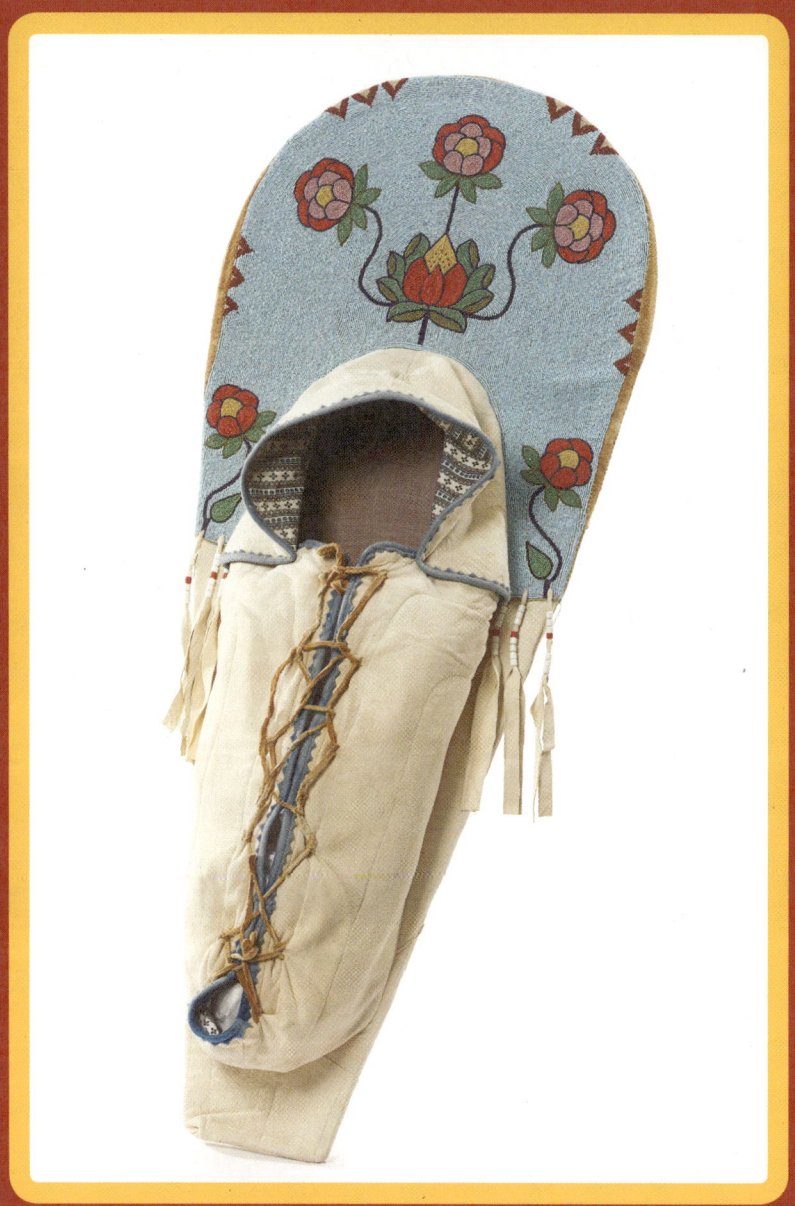

Cradleboard, mid-20th century.
Most of the Aboriginal peoples of North America used cradleboards to carry their babies until they were weaned and able to walk. The use of the cradleboard ensured that the baby was always with his or her mother and could be fed whenever hungry.

JANUARY

22   **1913.** The Nisga'a asserted their claim to land in the Nass River Valley, British Columbia.

23

24

25   **1841.** Grand Chief Pausauhmigh Pemmeenauweet of the Mi'kmaq wrote to Queen Victoria for help to alleviate starvation amongst his people.

26

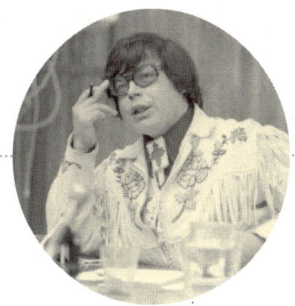

27   **1945.** Harold Cardinal, Cree leader and lawyer, was born on the Sucker Creek Reserve in Alberta. He is pictured here at a meeting of First Nations in Calgary, c. 1975. ▶

28   **2002.** The Métis Act, legislation meant to recognize Métis heritage and enable bilateral relations between Saskatchewan and the Métis Nation of Saskatchewan, was passed in the legislature.

Indian Residential Schools

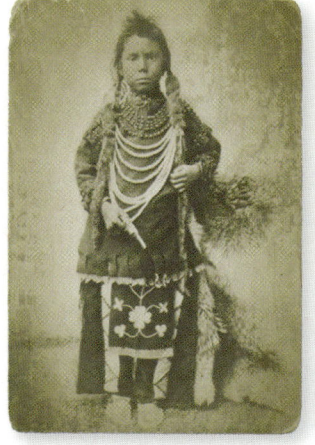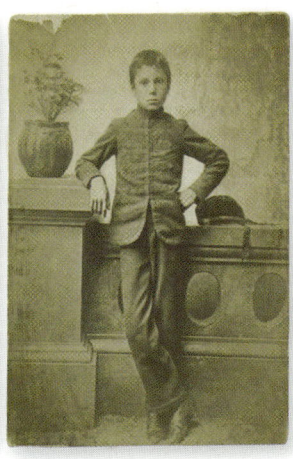

A staged photograph of a young Aboriginal boy before (left) and after (right) admission to the Regina Indian Residential School in 1897.

Treaties signed between the Queen as represented by the Canadian government and First Nations people included provisions regarding the education of children, but each side had its own vision for this education. First Nations people hoped that an education system created by the government would enable their children to succeed in the newcomer environment to which they were not accustomed. The government hoped that First Nations traditions and customs would diminish and be replaced by Euro-Canadian ways, thereby assimilating subsequent generations into Canadian society. The result of these differing visions was catastrophic. Three residential schools were opened in 1883, and by 1930 approximately 80 residential schools were operating across Canada—the outcome of a formal partnership between the Canadian government and Christian churches. In 1920, attendance was federally mandated, so children were brought to these institutions from their communities, and many were separated from their homes and families for years. The schools were run by missionaries, the majority representing the Roman Catholic Church, but there were also schools administered by Anglicans, Methodists and Presbyterians. Typically, students would spend half the day learning in a classroom, and the other half was spent working. Putting them to work, the missionaries believed, would reflect the working environments they would be expected to join when they left school. Students were also forbidden to speak their language, with the expectation that they would communicate only in English or French, and the study and work environments were gender segregated, so even if a brother and sister went to the same

JANUARY

 2009. The Legacy of Hope Foundation exhibit *"We Were So Far Away…": The Inuit Experience of Residential Schools* opened at Library and Archives Canada in Ottawa.

 1981. The draft Canadian Constitution was amended with a new sub-section stating that "the Aboriginal Peoples of Canada included Indian, Inuit, and Métis peoples"—thus officially recognizing the Métis as one of the First Peoples of Canada.

 1973. The Supreme Court ruled in *Calder v. Attorney General* that Aboriginal rights to land exist in law.

school, they would never see each other. Students were abused for any infraction, both emotionally and physically, and there have been many allegations of sexual abuse. Following their schooling, children returned to their homes traumatized, unable to function in their communities or in newcomer society. By the 1940s, both the government and many of the missionaries realized that the residential school "experiment" had failed. Despite this recognition, and protests from First Nations communities, no decision was made to actually terminate the residential schools agreement until 1969, and the last residential school was not closed until 1996. Efforts have since been made by the Canadian government, in concert with Catholic, Anglican, United and Presbyterian churches, to compensate First Nations people forced to attend the residential schools, and, in 2007, a $1.9-billion compensation package was formalized. In 2008, Stephen Harper, Prime Minister of Canada, apologized to those students on behalf of the government, but that may be cold comfort to the estimated 150,000 people forced to attend residential schools who had their education, culture and communities irrevocably damaged.

(JAMES OSTIME)

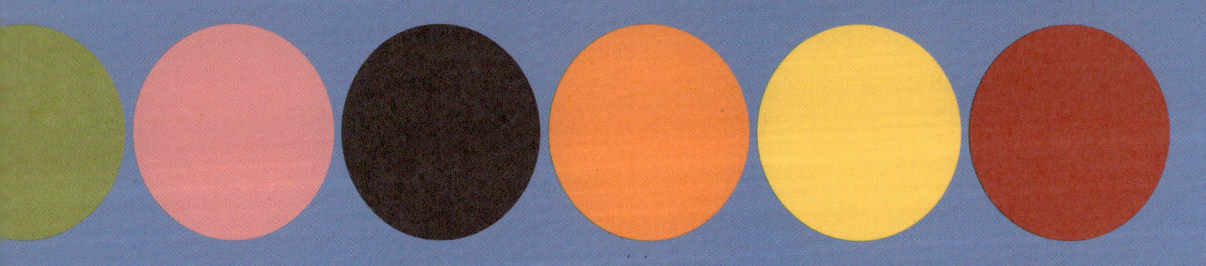

- **c. 12th century CE:** Aiionwatha, more commonly known as "Hiawatha," helped to establish the Haudenosaunee Confederacy, consisting of the Mohawk, Oneida, Seneca, Onondaga and Cayuga Nations (the Tuscarora Nation joined the Confederacy in 1722).

- **1728–29:** A Cree guide by the name of Auchagah prepared a map of canoe routes between Lakes Superior and Winnipeg for Pierre Gaultier de Varennes, Sieur de La Vérendrye, at what is now Thunder Bay, Ontario. La Vérendrye would use the map in his later explorations of northwestern North America.

- **1862–63:** Bands of the M'dewakontonwon and Wahpetonwon Dakota migrated to the Red River area of Manitoba, following the suppression of the Sioux Uprising in what is now Minnesota, USA.

- **1946** (February 24): 113 First Nations leaders from Saskatchewan met at Saskatoon to discuss political organization.

- **1999** (February 15): 19 legislators were elected to the first territorial government in Nunavut.

february

temt'emlémtses
(HALKOMELEM—CENTRAL SALISH)

"Time (things) stick to the hand (in the cold)"

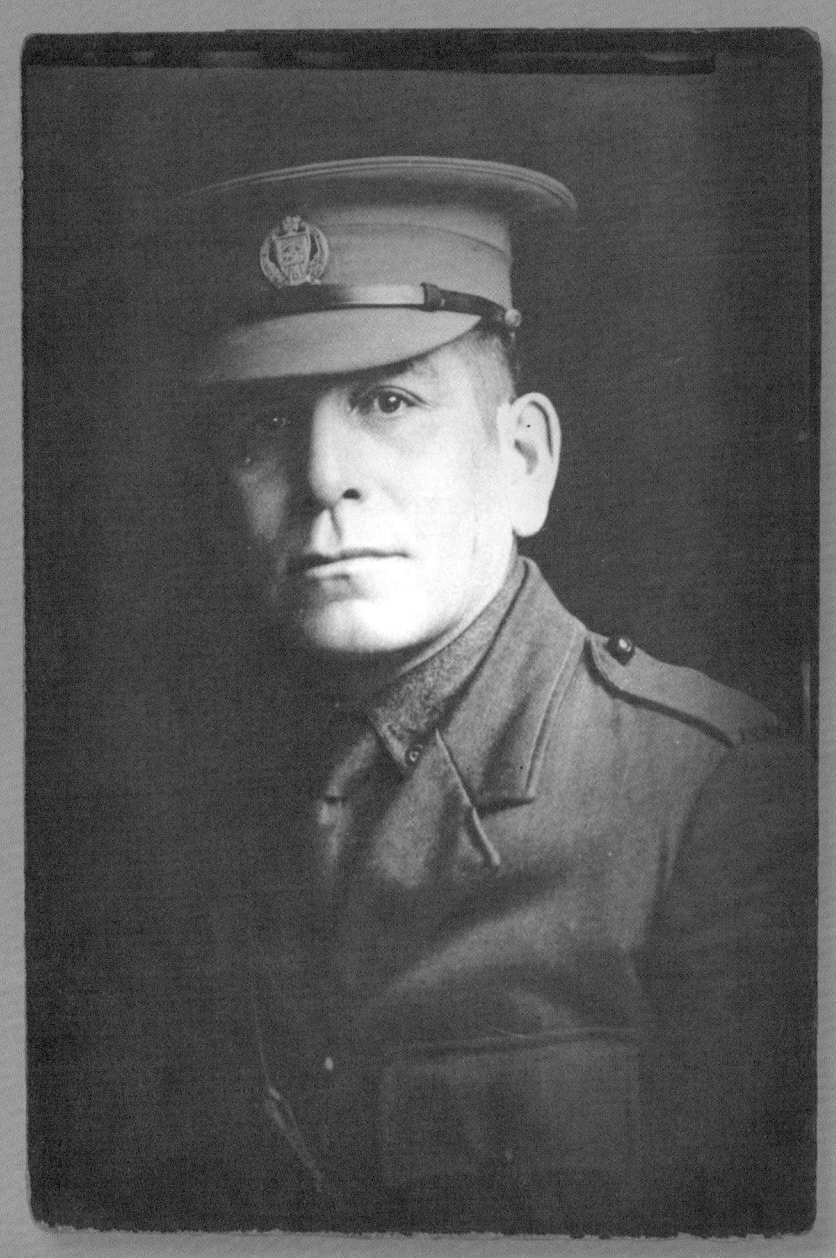

Lieutenant Frederick Ogilvie Loft, c. 1914–1918.
See February 3.

FEBRUARY

1

2 **1999.** The Aboriginal Peoples Television Network was licensed. ▶

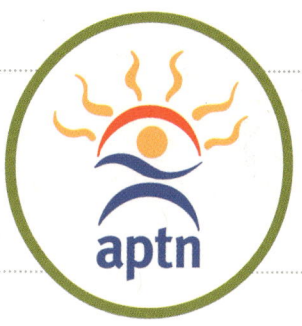

3 **1861.** Frederick Ogilvie Loft (Onondeyoh) of the Mohawk nation was born. Loft founded the League of Indians of Canada in 1918 and is considered one of the great Indian activists of the first half of the 20th century.

4

5 **1973.** Live colour television shows were delivered to northern provincial and territorial audiences for the first time.

6 **1892.** Andrew Paull, activist for the Salish people, was born at Squamish, British Columbia.

7

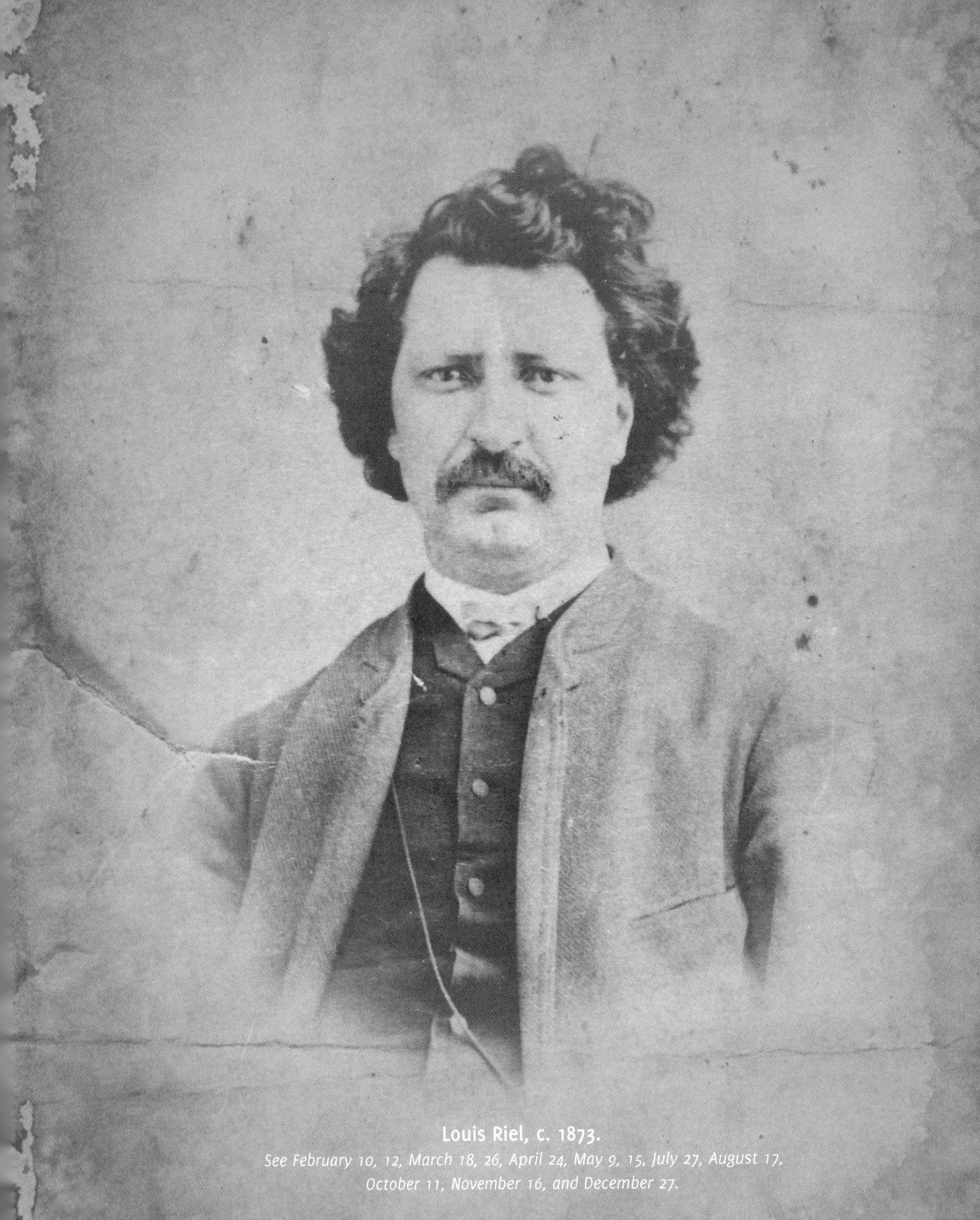

Louis Riel, c. 1873.
See February 10, 12, March 18, 26, April 24, May 9, 15, July 27, August 17, October 11, November 16, and December 27.

FEBRUARY

8

9 **1990.** Monique Mojica's *Princess Pocahontas and the Blue Spots* premiered at Theatre Passe Muraille, Toronto, Ontario.

10 **1870.** Louis Riel's provisional government was proclaimed with Riel as president. ▶

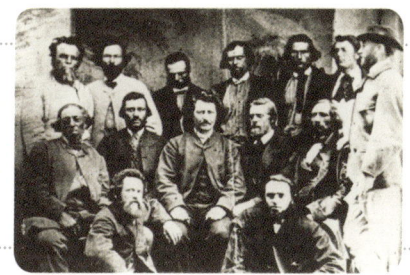

11 **1888.** Mary Augusta Tappage, Shuswap poet, was born at Soda Creek, British Columbia.

12 **1875.** Louis Riel was granted amnesty by Parliament for his role in the execution of Thomas Scott in 1870.

13 **1966.** Cree elders and dancers offered their last oblations to the buffalo rock, *mistasiniy*, in the Qu'Appelle Valley, Saskatchewan. ▶

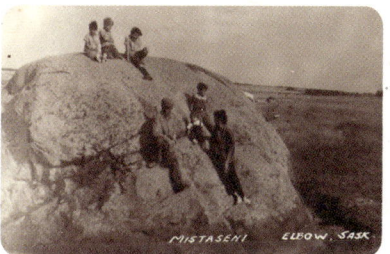

14 **1946.** The Association of Saskatchewan Indians and the Protective Association for Indians and their Treaties met at Saskatoon to form the Union of Saskatchewan Indians.

Buffy Sainte-Marie

Buffy Sainte-Marie is known globally as a First Nations composer, musician, actress, visual artist and educator, and her most celebrated contribution to pop culture has been her singing and songwriting. Her songs have been performed by many artists such as Elvis Presley, Barbra Streisand, and Cher, and her ballad, "Up Where We Belong," as performed by Joe Cocker and Jennifer Warnes, earned her an Academy Award in 1983. In addition to her commercial success, Sainte-Marie has been a public advocate of First Nations rights, which has earned her many accolades, and some backlash. Born in 1941 on the Piapot Reserve near Craven, Saskatchewan, she lost her parents as an infant and was adopted by a part-Mi'kmaw family, who raised her in Wakefield, Massachusetts. She retained her ties to the Piapot Reserve, though, when she was adopted in accordance with tribal custom by a Cree family who lived there and were related to her birth parents. Sainte-Marie gained attention as a singer-songwriter in the then thriving folk music scene in Canada, and Greenwich Village in New York. She became increasingly well-known in the 1960s but then found herself blacklisted by U.S. Presidents Lyndon Johnson and Richard Nixon. Johnson and Nixon believed that Sainte-Marie, along with other performers such as Taj Mahal and Eartha Kitt, "deserved to be suppressed." It was Sainte-Marie's criticism of the U.S. government's handling of the Siege at Wounded Knee in 1973 that kept her off the airwaves of U.S. radio stations. This siege ended with an armed battle with the U.S. army, and this conflict was protested by many public figures, including Sainte-Marie, hence her blacklisting. During that time, she became a cast member on the children's television program *Sesame Street*, where she remained for five years (1975-1980). Today, her output of music and visual art continues to be prolific. She has taught music and art at York University in Toronto, Evergreen State College in Olympia, Washington, the Institute for American Indian Arts in Santa Fe, New Mexico, and the Saskatchewan Indian Federated College, now the First Nations University of Canada, in Regina, Saskatchewan. (JAMES OSTIME)

FEBRUARY

15 **1997.** The Nova Scotia Native Women's Association held a conference on Aboriginal women and self-government.

16

17

18 **1981.** Federation of Métis Settlements President Elmer Ghostkeeper accepted the role of deputy chair of the Native Council of Canada's Métis and Non-Status Indian Constitutional Review Commission.

1992. The Privy Council ruled that elections held at Indian Brook First Nation for band councillors were invalid—the first time such a ruling had been made in Nova Scotia.

19

20 **1941.** Buffy Sainte-Marie, Cree singer/songwriter, was born on the Piapot Reserve in Saskatchewan. In 1982 she won an Academy Award for writing "Up Where You Belong," the theme for *An Officer and a Gentleman*. ▶

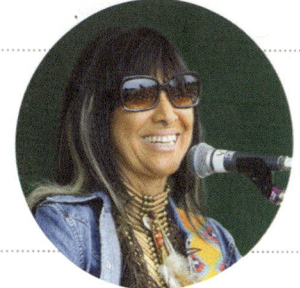

21 **1921.** George Manuel, National Chief of the Assembly of First Nations (1970–76), was born.

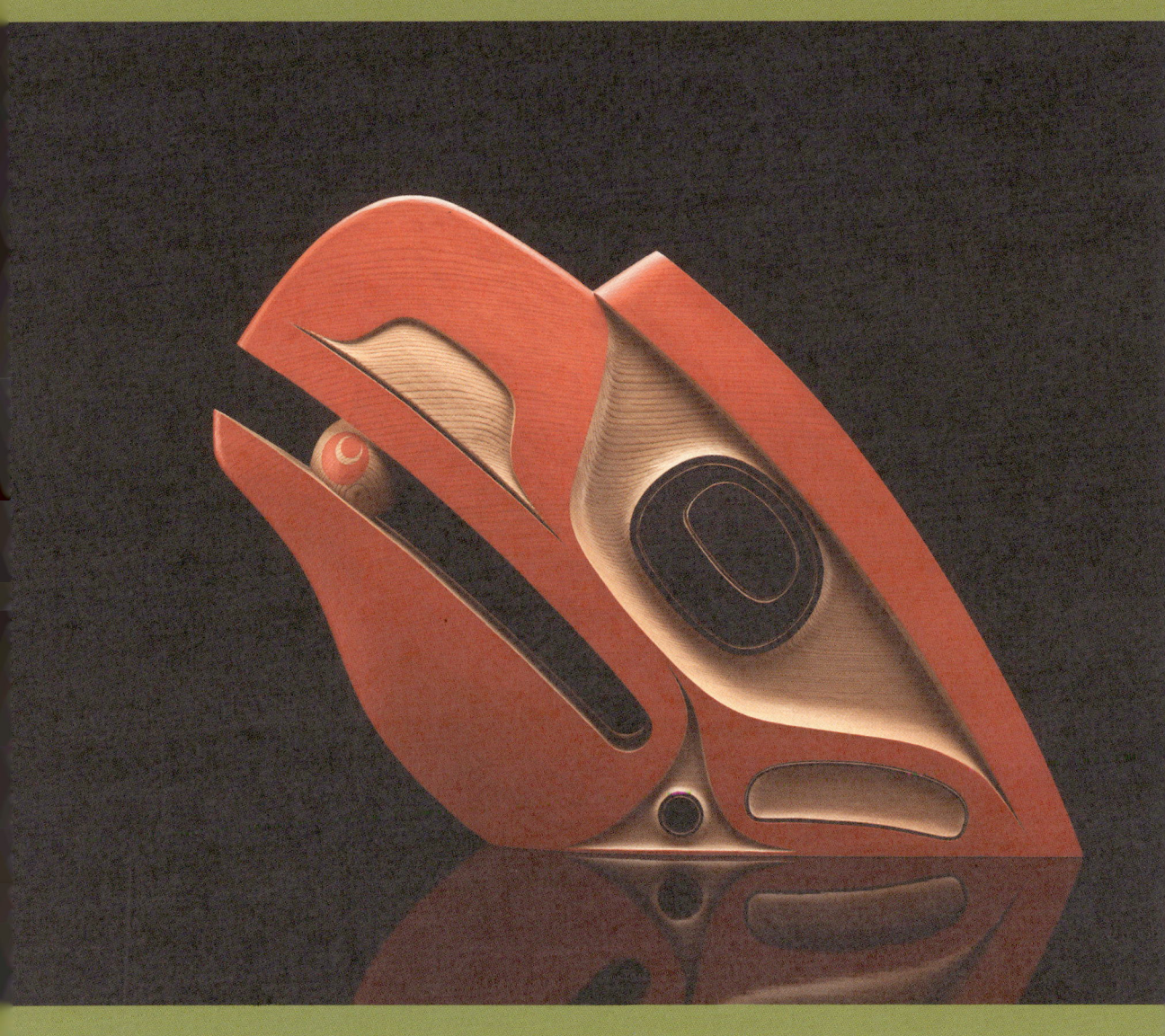

Robert Davidson, *Ravenous.*
Carved cedar sculpture, 2003.
See February 26 and November 4.

FEBRUARY

22 **1873.** The Government of Manitoba, under orders from Lieutenant-Governor Alexander Morris, began surveying 140-acre grants for Métis in Manitoba.

23 **2007.** The Assembly of First Nations and the First Nations Child & Family Caring Society filed a complaint with the Canadian Human Rights Commission over inadequate resourcing of First Nations Child and Family Services agencies.

24

25

26 **1997.** Internationally renowned Haida artist Robert Davidson, C.M., O.B.C., D.F.A. (Hon.), was invested as a Member of the Order of Canada.

27 **1988.** George Clutesi (b. 1905), Tseshaht artist, actor and writer, advocate of Native Canadian culture and member of the Order of Canada, died.

28/29 **1985.** Bill C-31, an amendment to the Indian Act, was introduced in Parliament, enabling women and children who lost their status through marriage to non-Status First Nations men to apply to regain it.

- **2011:** There are 51 (or 52) First Nation languages currently spoken in Canada, belonging to 11 language families.

- **2011:** Cree has the largest number of speakers, approximately 115,000, with nine dialects.

- **2011:** Ojibwe has the second largest number of speakers, approximately 48,000, with seven dialects.

- **2011:** Inuktitut has the third largest number of speakers, approximately 35,000, with 12 (or 13) dialects.

- **2011:** Kutenai appears to be the most endangered First Nation language, with only 120 speakers.

march

sa'áíki'somma
(BLACKFOOT)
"Duck Moon"

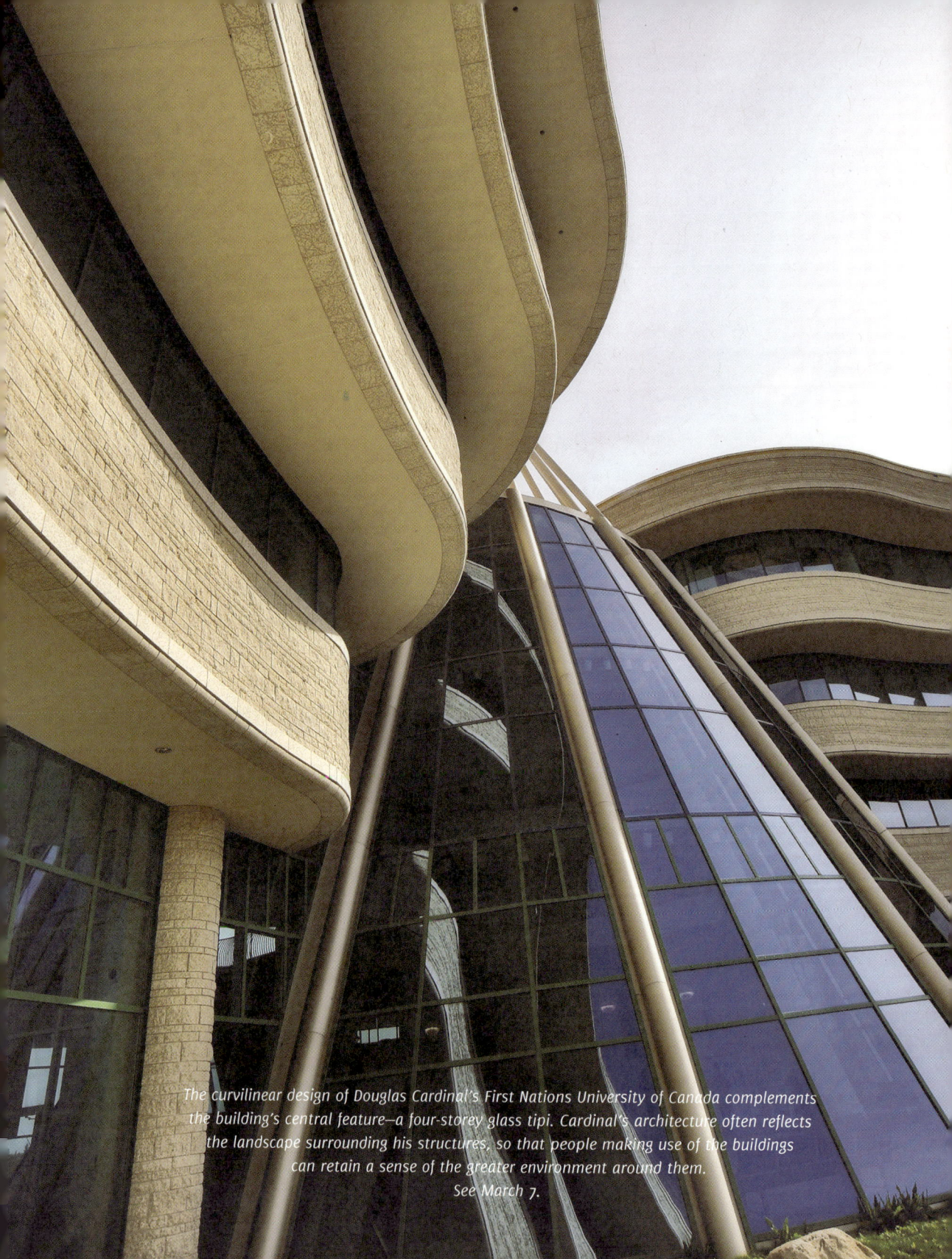

The curvilinear design of Douglas Cardinal's First Nations University of Canada complements the building's central feature—a four-storey glass tipi. Cardinal's architecture often reflects the landscape surrounding his structures, so that people making use of the buildings can retain a sense of the greater environment around them.
See March 7.

MARCH

1 **1997.** Dr. Oliver Brass, Saskatchewan Indian Federated College President and first Ph.D. graduate amongst Saskatchewan First Nations, died.

2 **1998.** Lee-Ann Martin, Mohawk, was appointed Native Head Curator of Mackenzie Art Gallery, Regina, Saskatchewan.

1871. Angus McKay (Marquette, Manitoba) became the first person of Métis ancestry elected to the Canadian House of Commons.

3 **1960.** A Dominion Order-in-Council divided the single Mi'kmaw Band of Nova Scotia into eleven bands with assigned reserve lands.

4

5 **1993.** Yvon Dumont became the first member of Manitoba's Métis community to be appointed Lieutenant-Governor of Manitoba.

1980. Jay Silverheels, Mohawk, best known for his role as Tonto on *The Lone Ranger*, died.

6 **1998.** The Kainai (Blood) Tribe and the Glenbow Museum in Calgary, Alberta, agreed to work together on matters of First Nations art, the first agreement of its kind in Canada.

7 **1934.** Douglas Joseph Cardinal, Blackfoot/Métis architect, was born at Red Deer, Alberta. ▶

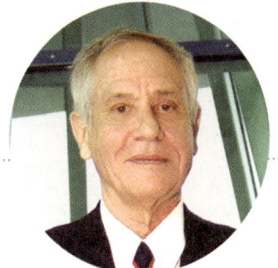

Pauline Johnson and "The Legend of the Qu'Appelle Valley"

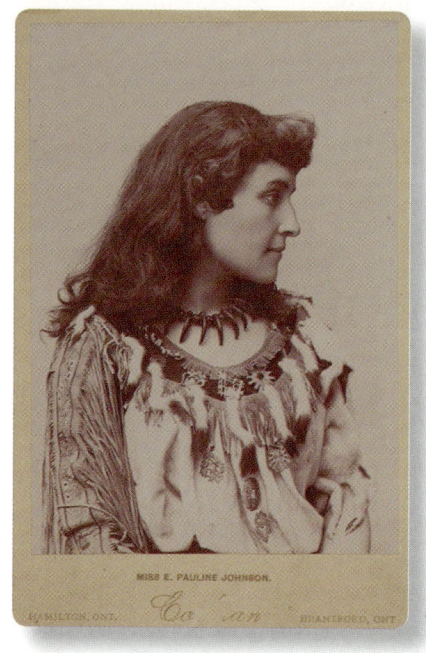

Emily Pauline Johnson was born in 1861 at the Six Nations Reserve in British-controlled Canada West. Her mother was a U.S. citizen originally from England, and her father was a Six Nations Mohawk Chief. Johnson was a prominent poet, writer and entertainer who performed across Canada to such acclaim and audiences that she was able to support herself financially as a result of these artistic endeavours, a rarity for women of that time, particularly those of First Nations descent. She was known professionally first as Pauline Johnson, then by her grandfather's ancestral name, Tekahionwake, in honour of her First Nations heritage. She further embraced her ancestry by beginning her public performances in contemporary European clothing, then changing into traditional buckskin. Her work also dealt with First Nations people and themes in a distinctly Canadian context. One of her most well-known and celebrated pieces is "The Legend of the Qu'Appelle Valley." The poem tells of a young man canoeing home from a hunt and hearing a voice calling his name. "Who calls?" he asks, and receives no answer, and his question ("*Kâ-têpwêt?*" in Cree and "*Qui appelle?*" in French) echoes back to him through the valley. The young man returns home the next evening to find that the young maiden he was to marry had died the night before and, with her dying breath, had called his name. This poem retold the legend first reported by Métis trader Daniel Harmon in the early 19th century, when First Nations inhabitants of the region claimed to hear voices as they travelled through the valley. They would respond, "Who calls?", "*Kâ-têpwêt?*" and "*Qui appelle?*" Johnson died in 1913; her work has been republished in several anthologies, and many First Nations writers today cite her as an important influence. (JAMES OSTIME)

MARCH

8   **1983.** In Regina, the provincial Métis organizations established the Métis National Council. The first action was to announce their intention to seek an injunction to stall any First Ministers Conferences on constitutional matters that did not provide two voting seats for Métis representatives.

9

10   **1861.** Tekahionwake (Pauline Johnson) was born on the Six Nations Reserve, Canada West (now Ontario).

11   **1989.** Na Gaisgich (Douglas) Brown, Patrick Johnson, Eleanor (née Paul) Johnson, and Joe B. Marshall, Mi'kmaw students, were inducted into the University College of Cape Breton Honours Society.

12   **2011.** Olive Patricia Dickason, renowned Métis journalist, scholar and author, died at the age of 91.

     2002. Edward Poitras was among the winners of the annual Governor General's Awards in Visual and Media Arts. In 1995, he was the first Aboriginal artist to represent Canada at the Venice Biennale. ▼

13   **1978.** Mi'kmaw Helen Martin received an award from the Province of Nova Scotia for outstanding volunteer service to her community.

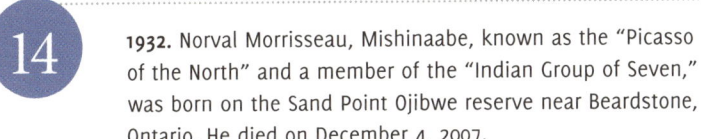

14   **1932.** Norval Morrisseau, Mishinaabe, known as the "Picasso of the North" and a member of the "Indian Group of Seven," was born on the Sand Point Ojibwe reserve near Beardstone, Ontario. He died on December 4, 2007.

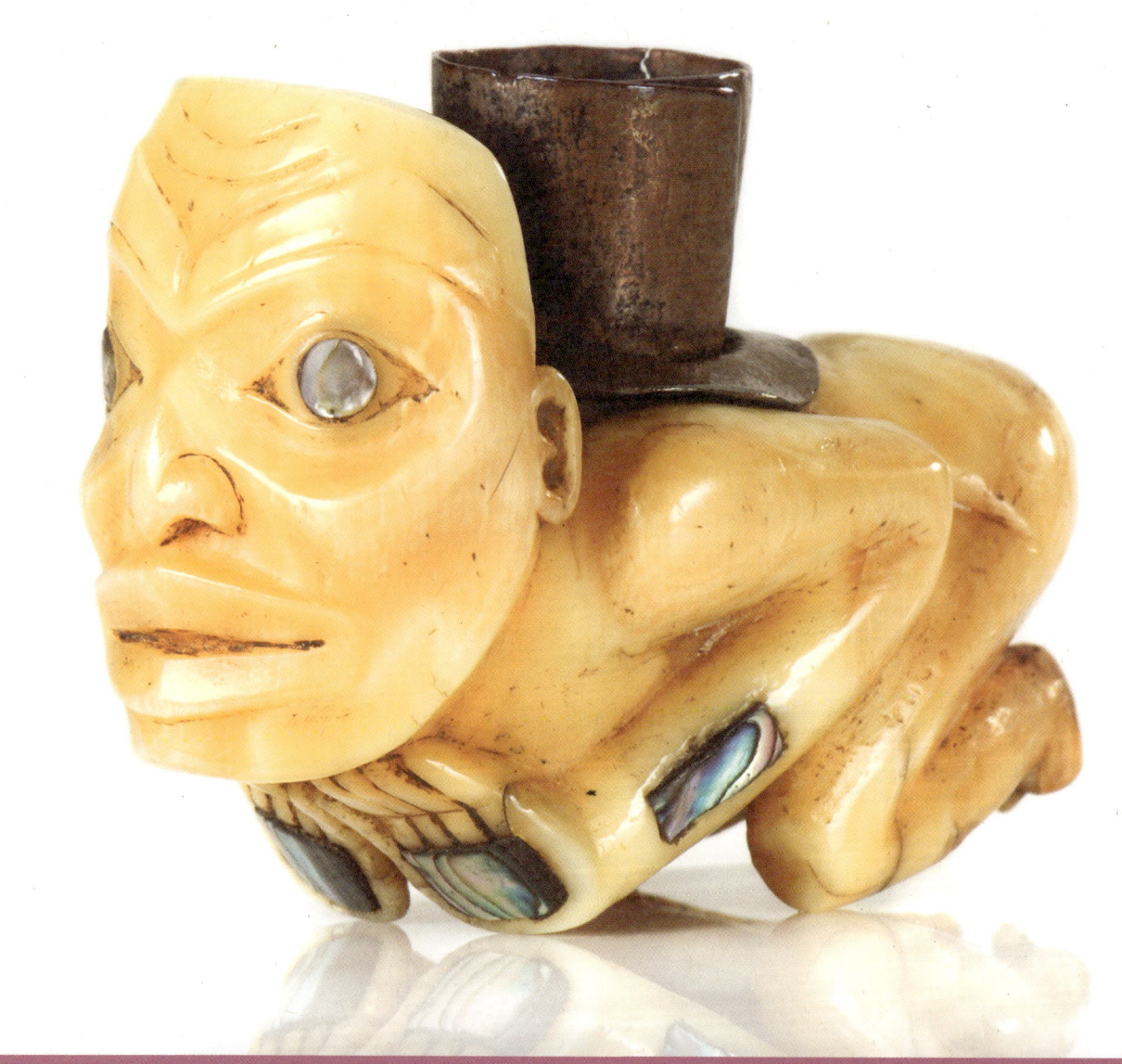

Tlingit pipe.
*Walrus ivory, abalone, copper, c. 1830s.
Elaborately carved pipes such as this one might have been smoked on ceremonial occasions
or possibly made for sale to tourists. The pipe bowl is lined with copper to protect the ivory.*

MARCH

15 — **1932.** Rita Joe, Mi'kmaw poet, was born in Whycocomogh, Cape Breton, Nova Scotia.

16

17 — **2003.** Supreme Court of Canada heard *R. v. Powley*, which determined whether Métis at Sault Ste. Marie had an Aboriginal right to hunt; the Powleys were represented by Arthur Pape and Jean Teillet. The Métis National Council and the Métis Nation of Ontario intervened on behalf of the Powleys; the interveners were represented by Clément Chartier and Jason Madden.

18 — **1885.** Métis formed the Provisional Government of Saskatchewan under leader Louis Riel.

19 — **1842.** Nova Scotia's legislature passed the Act for the Instruction and Permanent Settlement of Indians.

20 — **1962.** Tina Keeper, Cree actress and former Member of Parliament, was born.

21

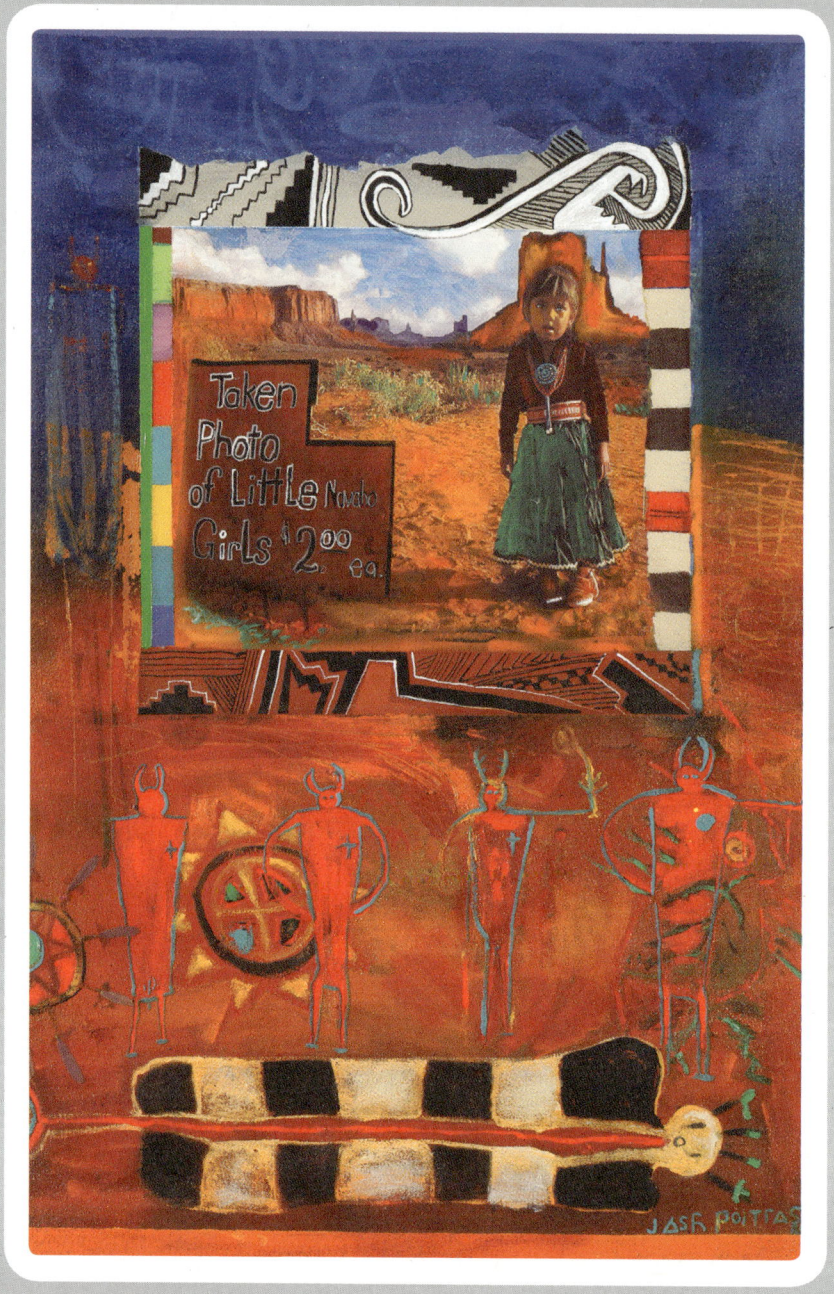

Jane Ash Poitras, *Two Dollars Please.*
Photograph and oil paint on canvas, 24 x 36 inches, 2004.
See April 9.

MARCH

22 — **2007.** Courts in seven jurisdictions approved the Indian Residential Schools Settlement Agreement.

23 — **1978.** Nicholas de Grandmaison (named Enuksapop – "Little Plume"), painter, died.

24

25 — **1951.** Ethel Blondin, Dene, who in 1988 became the first Aboriginal woman elected to the Canadian House of Commons, was born in Tulita, Northwest Territories.

26 — **1885.** The first encounter between Louis Riel's resistance force and North-West Mounted Police and civilian volunteers took place at Duck Lake, North-West Territories. ▶

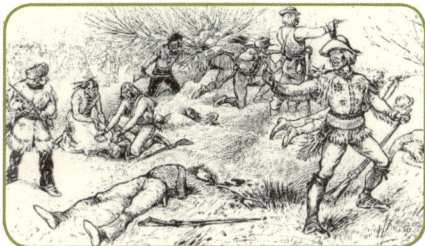

27 — **1982.** The Wagnatcook Mi'kmaw Band was the first in Atlantic Canada to settle a specific claim, and was rewarded $1.2 million for land improperly taken from its reserve.

28 — **1993.** The Saulteaux First Nation in Saskatchewan held a ratification vote on its Treaty Land Entitlement Framework Agreement.

First Nations, Inuit, and Métis Members of Parliament

Though Status First Nations people in Canada were not granted full federal voting rights until 1960, there have been First Nations, Métis, and Inuit Members of Parliament (MPs) since 1870, when Angus McKay, a Conservative Métis, was elected in Manitoba. Since, there have been 27 MPs who have been First Nations, Métis, or Inuit— besides McKay, 14 have been Métis. Five MPs were Inuit, the first of whom was Peter Ittinuar, a member of the NDP, elected in the Northwest Territories (NWT) in 1979. Eight MPs have been First Nations, beginning with Len Marchand, a Liberal, elected in 1968. There have been 5 female MPs, beginning with Ethel Blondin-Andrew, a Dene from NWT, elected in 1988. Twelve of these MPs were Liberals, 10 Conservative, or Progressive-Conservative, 4 members of the NDP, one (Bernard Cleary of Quebec) was with the Bloc Québécois, and one ran as an Independent in 1873—the Métis leader, Louis Riel. As of 2011, there is one First Nations MP serving, Saskatchewan Conservative Rob Clarke. There are 3 Métis: Todd Norman Russell, a Liberal from Newfoundland and Labrador, and Rod Bruinooge and Shelly Glover, both Conservatives from Manitoba. Leona Aglukkaq, a Nunavut Conservative, serves as Canada's first Inuk member of Cabinet. (JAMES OSTIME)

PARLIAMENTARY FIRSTS

- Full federal voting rights were granted to Canada's Native peoples in 1960
- Ethel Blondin-Andrew, Dene, first Aboriginal woman Member of Parliament (1988)
- Angus McKay, first Métis Member of Parliament (1871)
- Peter Ittinuar, first Inuk Member of Parliament (1979)
- Leonard Marchand, Okanagan, first Member of Parliament of First Nation ancestry (1968)
- Nancy Karetak-Lindell, first Inuk woman Member of Parliament (1997)
- Leona Aglukkaq, first Inuk member of Cabinet (2008)

MARCH

29   **2004.** A delegation of Provincial Métis Women's organizations elected Rosemarie Macpherson as their national spokesperson.

30   **1931.** Chief Ben Pictou of the Bear River First Nation in Nova Scotia died at age 100 years.

31   **2001.** Mi'kmaw Justice of the Peace Daniel N. Paul was appointed to the Nova Scotia Police Commission.

"Let us put our minds together and see what life we will make for our children."

—NOEL STARBLANKET, STARBLANKET FIRST NATION

- **1638–1698:** The "Beaver Wars" (also known as the "Iroquois Wars") raged in eastern North America. Control of the fur trade lay behind the series of conflicts, which saw the near total destruction of the Neutral, Erie, Susquehannock, Wenro, and Huron peoples at the hands of the Iroquois Confederacy.

- **c. 1640:** The Assiniboine are believed to have split off from the Yanktonai Sioux, from their ancestral homeland at the headwaters of the Mississippi River.

- **1690–1691:** Henry Kelsey was the first European to encounter the Assiniboine during his explorations on behalf of the Hudson's Bay Company.

- **1823:** Shanawdithit (Beothuk) and her family, were found in dire circumstances by settlers in Newfoundland.

april
tabehatawi
(ASSINIBOINE)

"Frog Moon"

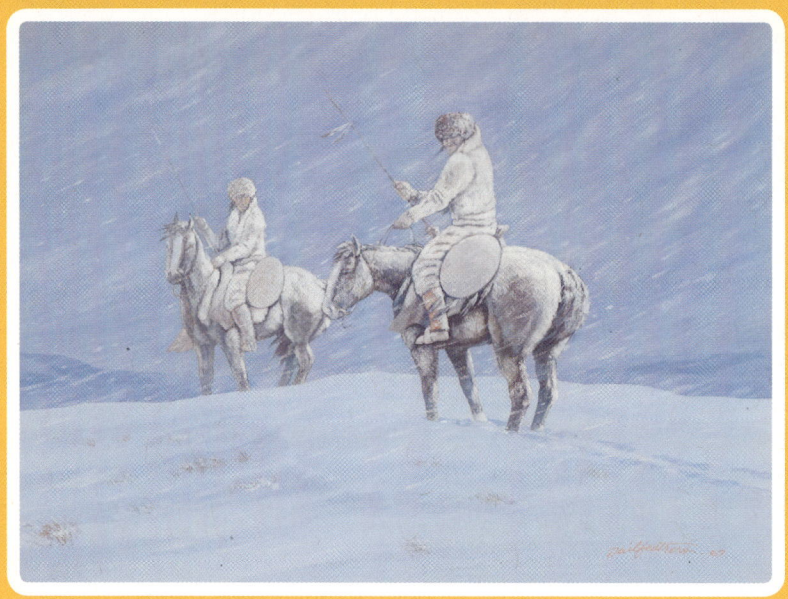

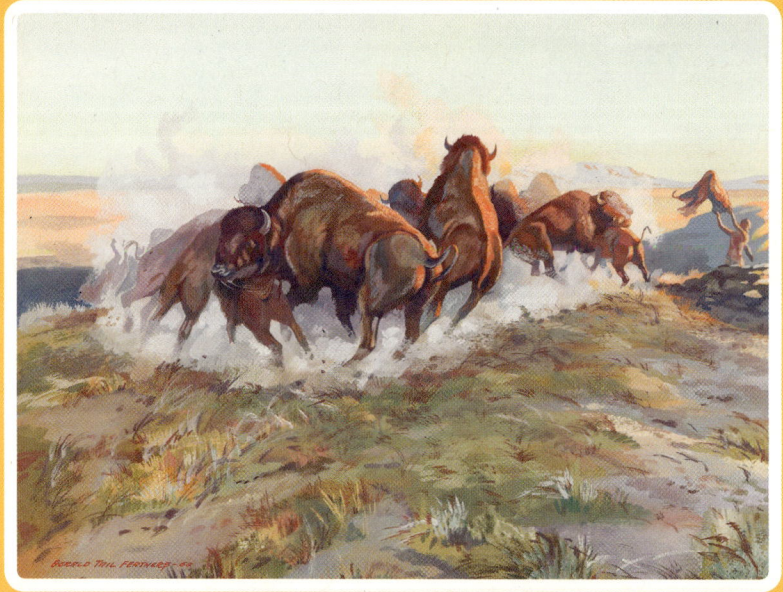

Gerald Tailfeathers,
(top) Blizzard. *Oil on canvas, 1967;*
(bottom) The Kill. *Tempera on paper, 1960.*
See April 3.

APRIL

1 **1999.** Nunavut ("Our Land" in Inuktitut) became Canada's third territory.

2 **1885.** Non-Aboriginal settlers were killed at Frog Lake, North-West Territories (in present-day Alberta), by followers of Big Bear. The names of the dead were inscribed on a large cross in the middle of a burial site, which was surrounded by smaller unmarked wooden crosses. ▼

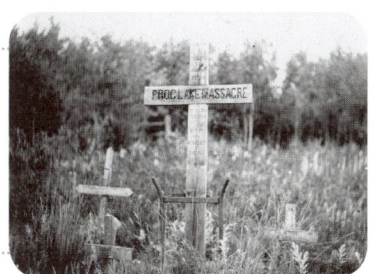

3 **1975.** Gerald Tailfeathers, Kainai (Blood) artist, died on the Blood Reserve, Alberta.

4 **1909.** Harry Gabriel Chonkolay, the last hereditary chief in Alberta, was born at Meander River, Alberta.

5 **1832.** Peter Jones, the first Ojibwe to be ordained a Methodist minister, had an audience with King William IV. ▶

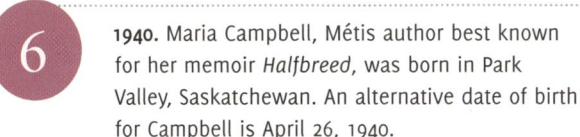

6 **1940.** Maria Campbell, Métis author best known for her memoir *Halfbreed*, was born in Park Valley, Saskatchewan. An alternative date of birth for Campbell is April 26, 1940.

7

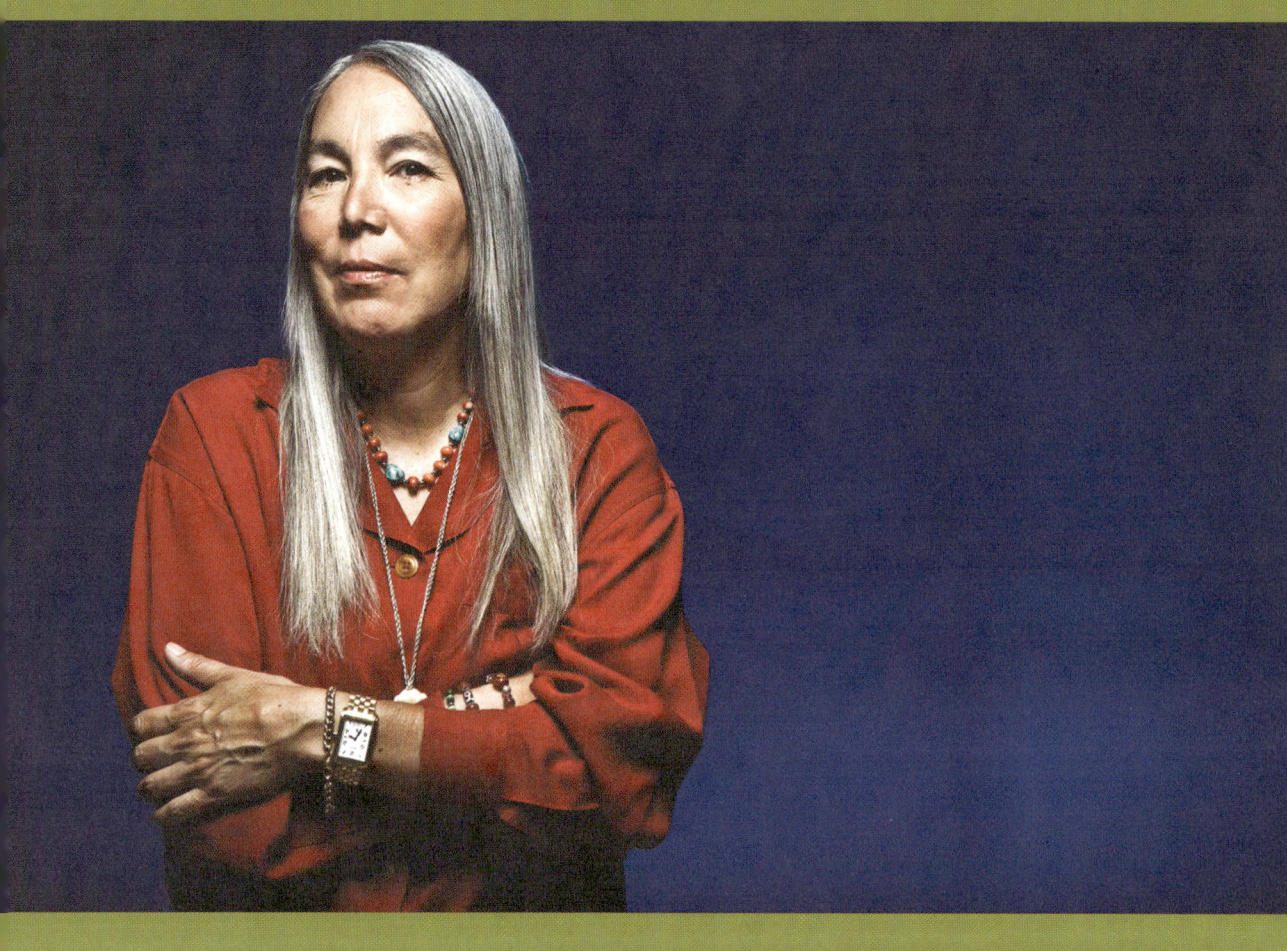

Jane Ash Poitras.
See April 9.

APRIL

8

9 — **2011.** Internationally renowned Aboriginal artist Jane Ash Poitras was presented with the Lieutenant-Governor of Alberta's Distinguished Artist Award.

10 — **1915.** David Knight, future chief of the Federation of Saskatchewan Indian Nations, was born at Moose Lake Mountain.

11

12 — **1885.** Big Bear helped settlers escape Fort Pitt, North-West Territories.

13 — **1852.** An Order-in-Council transferred authority over all Aboriginal lands in Nova Scotia to the office of the Commissioner of Crown Lands for the Province.

14 — **1982.** District of Mackenzie voters rejected division of the Northwest Territories but were outvoted by the predominantly Inuit voters of the Districts of Franklin and Keewatin.

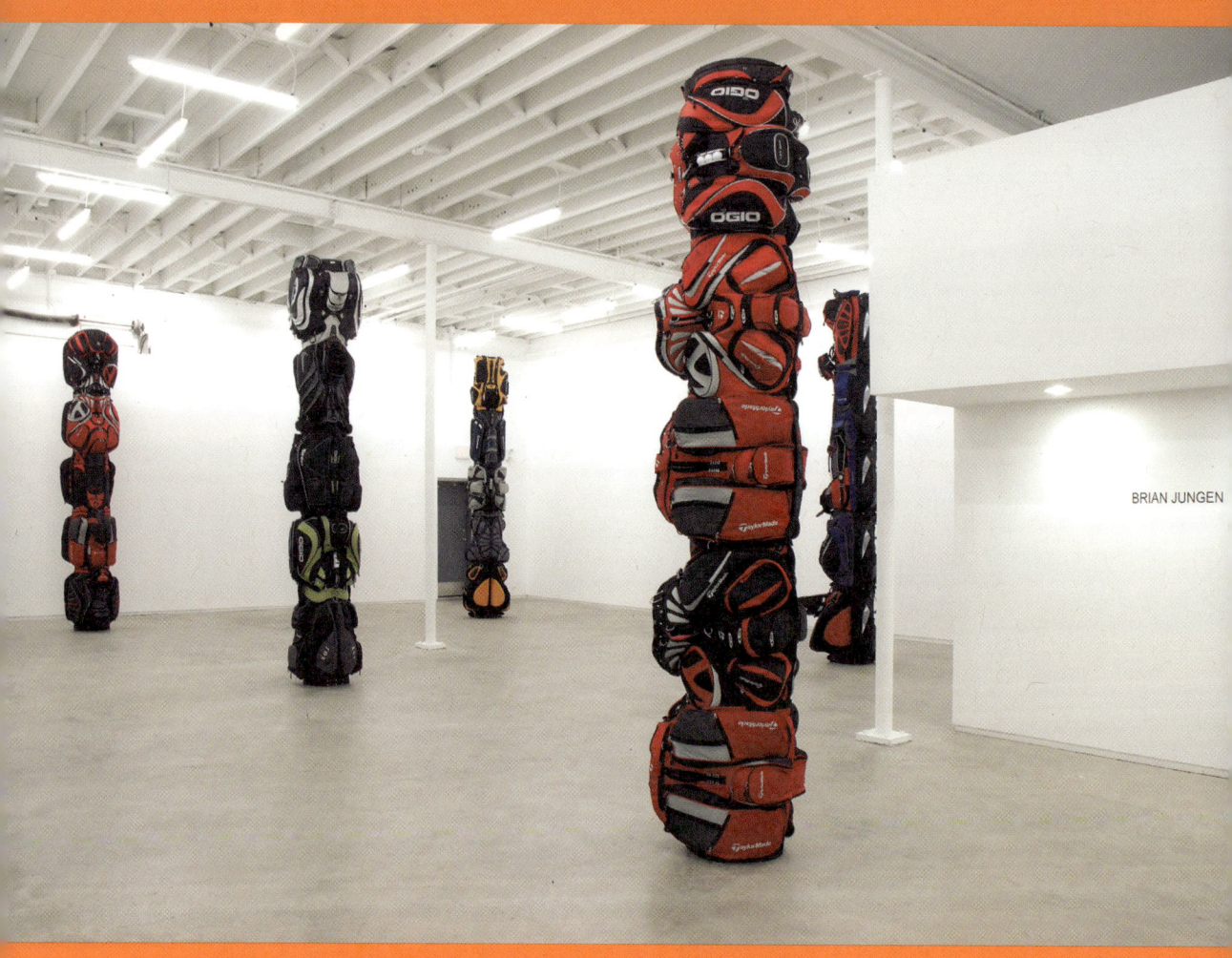

Brian Jungen.
Golf bags, cardboard tubes.
Installation view, Catriona Jeffries Gallery, Vancouver, 2007.
See April 29.

APRIL

15 **1977.** The Berger Enquiry called for a 10-year moratorium on pipeline construction in the Mackenzie Valley to allow time for First Nations and Inuit to settle land claims and prepare for developmental change.

16 **1982.** Status First Nation Chiefs formed the Federation of Saskatchewan Indian Nations (FSIN), the first Indian Legislative Assembly in Canada.

17 **1982.** Queen Elizabeth II, at the patriation ceremony in Ottawa, declared that the draft Constitution recognizing First Nations, Inuit, and Métis as the three Aboriginal peoples of Canada was legal.

18 **1990.** Mi'kmaw poet Rita Joe was inducted into the Order of Canada for her literary work.

19 **1907.** Tom Longboat, Onondaga athlete from the Six Nations Reserve, Ontario, won the Boston Marathon.

20 **1769.** Pontiac, chief of the Ottawa Indians, was murdered by a Peoria chief. ▶

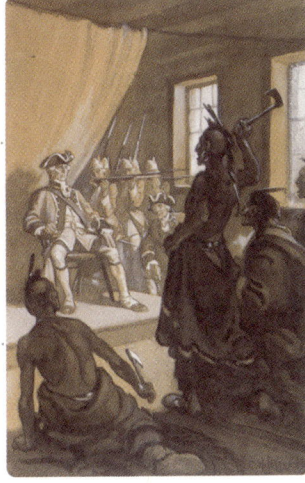

21 **1982.** Chief David Ahenakew was elected to replace Del Riley as president of National Indian Brotherhood/Assembly of First Nations.

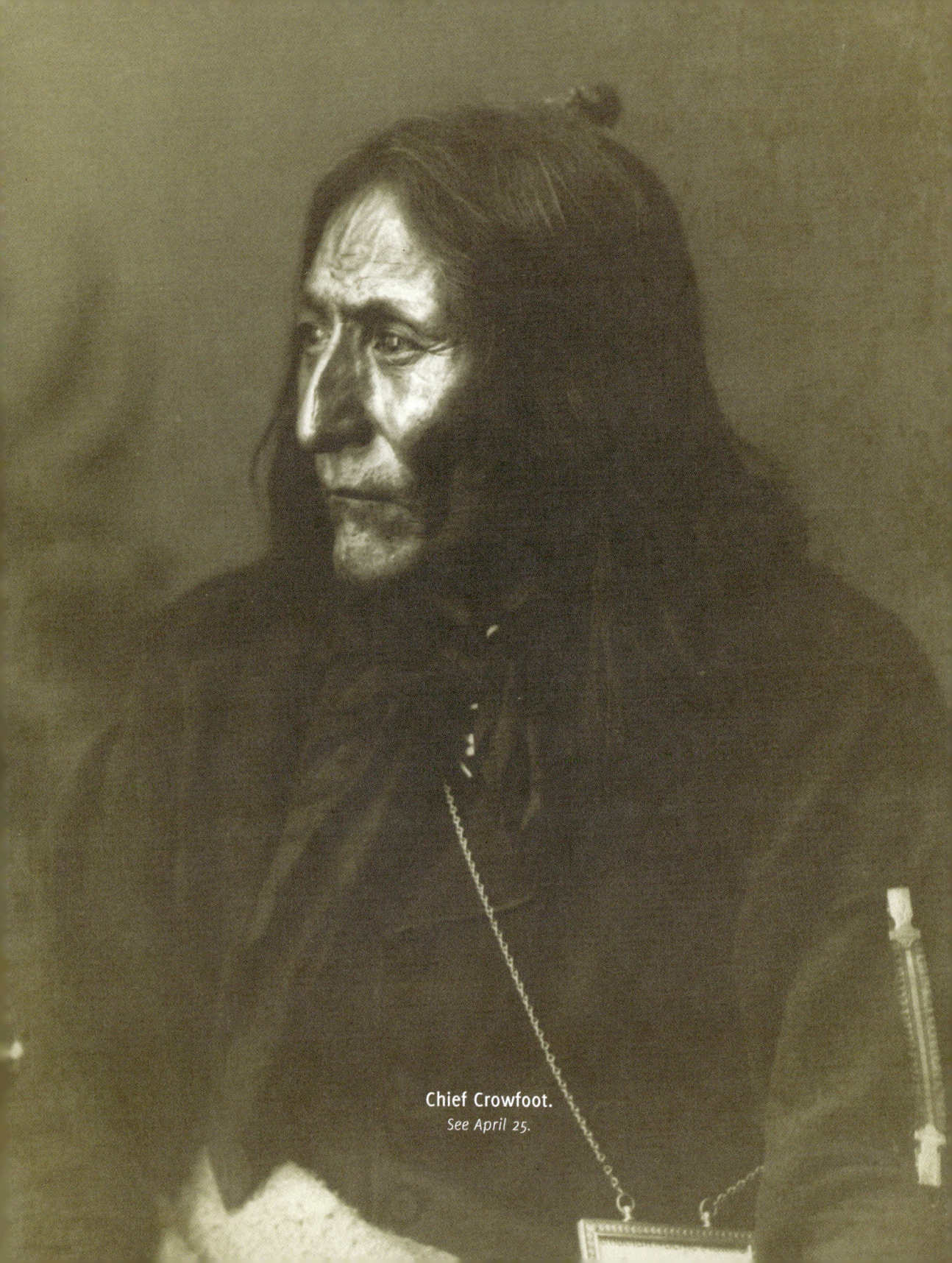

Chief Crowfoot.
See April 25.

APRIL

22   **1839.** James Buchanan Macauley, Canada West Judge, recommended that First Nations be assimilated rather than sent to reserves.

23   **1996.** The Royal Commission on Aboriginal Peoples released its five-volume report.

24   **1885.** Major General Frederick Middleton encountered Riel Resistance forces at Tourond's Coulee.

25   **1890.** Isapo-muxika, Blackfoot Chief Crowfoot, died near Blackfoot Crossing, Alberta, age 60.

26   **1875.** A federal government Order-in-Council announced it would take applicants for a Métis lands lottery in Manitoba.

27

28   **2008.** Indian and Northern Affairs Minister Chuck Strahl announced the appointment of Justice Harry LaForme, a member of the Mississaugas of the New Credit First Nation, as Chair of the Truth and Reconciliation Commission.

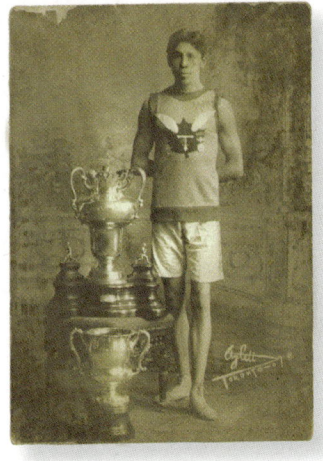 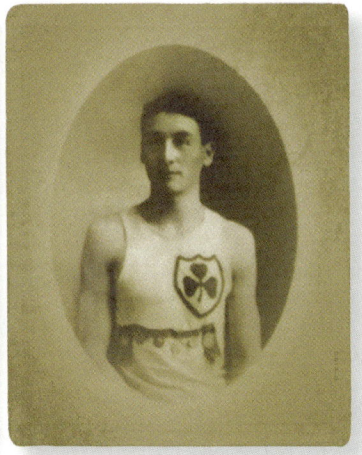 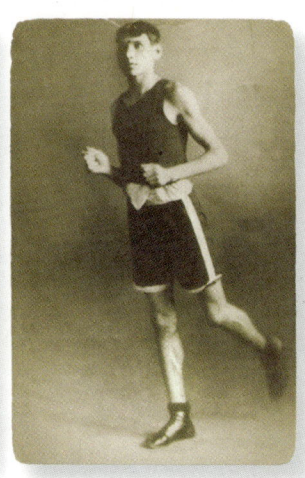

left to right: Tom Longboat, Alex Decoteau, and Paul Acoose

THE RUNNERS

In the early decades of the 20th century, three young Aboriginal Canadian men were among the best long-distance runners in the world: Paul Acoose (Saulteaux), Alex Decoteau (Cree) and Tom Longboat (Onondaga).

Paul Acoose (c. 1885-1978) was born in the Qu'Appelle Valley, in the North-West Territories. During his first race as a professional, Acoose defeated famed English runner Fred Appleby in a 15-mile race in a record time of 1:22:22. In a rematch a week later, a gambling enthusiast threw thumbtacks on the race track; and although Acoose completed the race with thumbtacks piercing his feet, he finished second. Although he ran many professional races, one of his proudest victories as a runner occurred on March 30, 1910, when he competed against Tom Longboat, whom he regarded as a superb athlete and his only match. After defeating Longboat, Acoose retired from running.

Alex Decoteau (December 1887-October 30, 1917) was born on the Red Pheasant Reserve near Battleford, North-West Territories. In 1912, he tried out for the Canadian Olympic team, setting a new Dominion record (5,000 m) at 15:27.4. At the Stockholm Summer Olympic Games later that year, Decoteau placed sixth in the 5,000-metre race, and was awarded an Olympic Merit Diploma and a medal

APRIL

 1970: Internationally renowned Canadian artist Brian Jungen was born in Fort St. John, British Columbia. Of Swiss and Dunne-za descent, Jungen was the recipient of the 2010 Gershon Iskowitz Prize at the Art Gallery of Ontario for his outstanding contribution to visual arts in Canada.

 1980. Federal Minister of Energy Marc Lalonde promised Status First Nations representation at constitutional conferences when matters pertaining to Aboriginal rights surfaced.

for his performance. In 1916 Decoteau joined the Canadian Army, winning several races while stationed in England. He was killed near Passchendaele Ridge in Belgium on October 30, 1917.

Tom Longboat (June 4, 1887-January 9, 1949) was born on the Six Nations of the Grand River First Nation Reserve near Brantford, Ontario. He won the Boston Marathon in 1907, and in 1908 he became the first Aboriginal Canadian to participate in the Olympics, attending the Summer Olympic Games in London, England. Longboat and several other competitors collapsed from heat during the Olympic Marathon, and a rematch was held the following year in New York, which Longboat won. In 1912, he set a record for the 15-mile run on Toronto Island, which still stands.

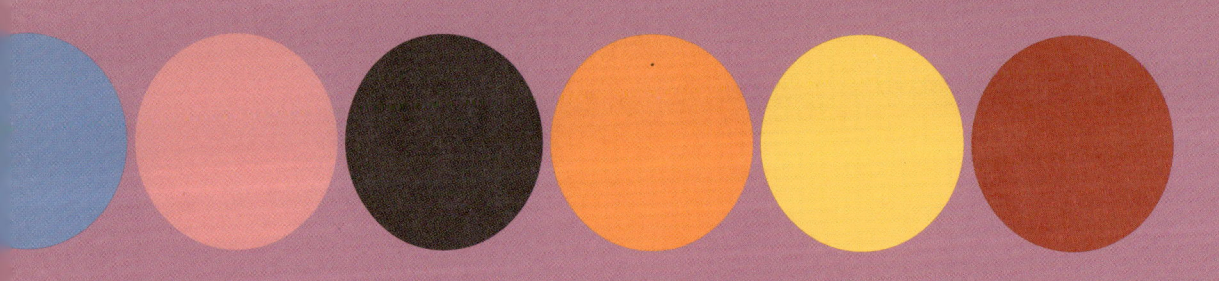

- **1604** (May 1): Samuel de Champlain arrived on the coast of Nova Scotia and made contact with the Mi'kmaq.

- **1640:** The first reference to the Cree appears in the *Jesuit Relations* of that year. The Jesuits referred to the Cree as Kiristinon.

- **c. 1740:** The Plains Cree begin moving onto the prairies, from their ancestral homeland in the Hudson's Bay area, as part of the steady expansion of the fur trade.

- **2008:** The Government of Ontario and the Grassy Narrows First Nation reach an agreement to end the roadblock of the Whiskey Jack Forest, which began in December 2002.

sākipakāwi-pīsim
(PLAINS CREE)

"Leaf-Budding Moon"

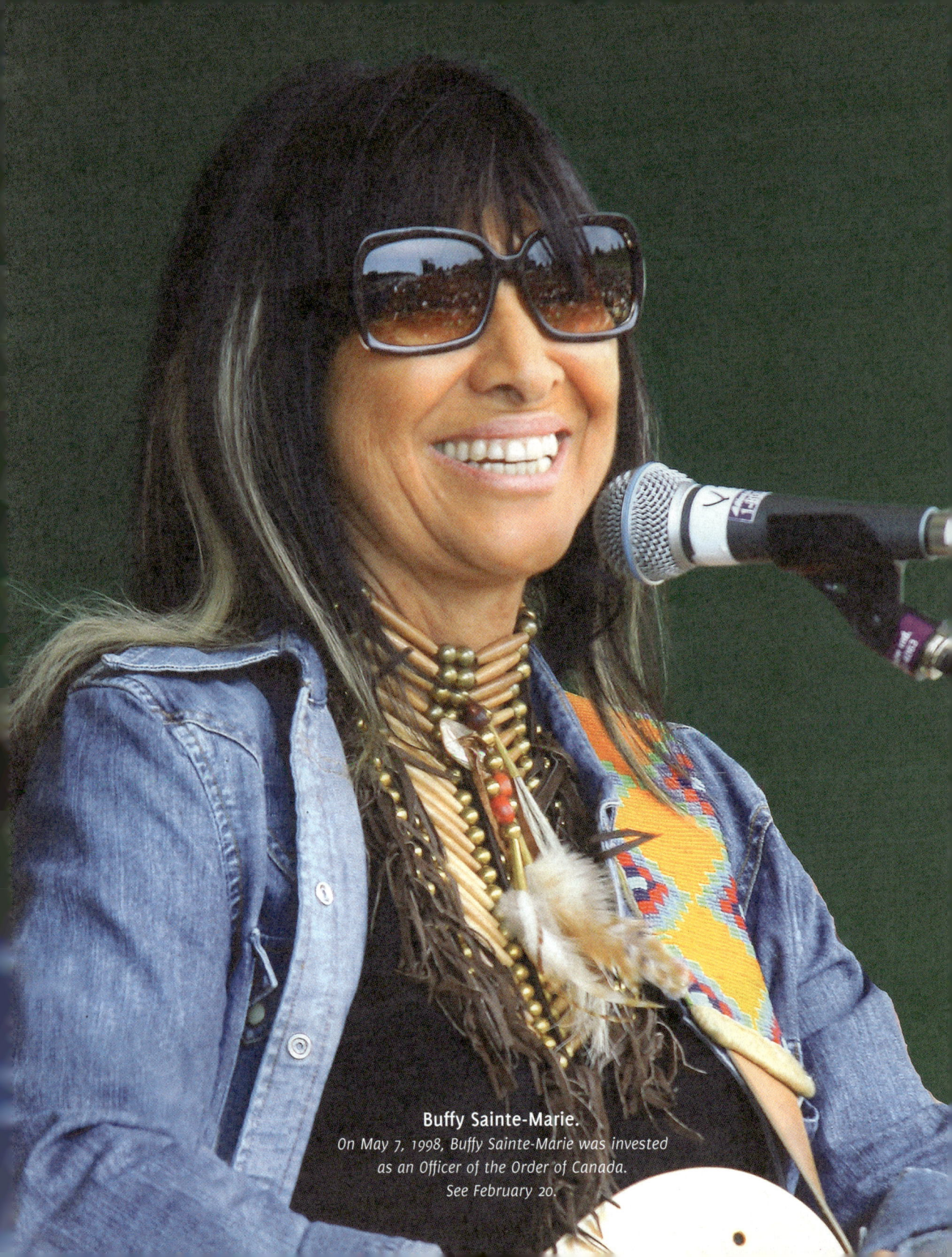

Buffy Sainte-Marie.
On May 7, 1998, Buffy Sainte-Marie was invested
as an Officer of the Order of Canada.
See February 20.

MAY

1 **2006.** The General Council Executive of the United Church of Canada agreed to sign the multi-party Indian Residential Schools Settlement Agreement.

2 **1950.** Jose A. Kusugak, future President of Inuit Tapiriit Kanatami, was born at Naujaat (Repulse Bay), Northwest Territories. He is pictured here (far right) at age 3. ▶

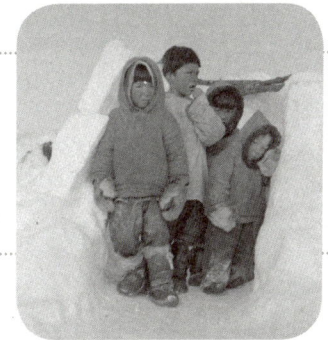

3 **1972.** The Cree and Inuit of northern Quebec filed for a permanent injunction to halt construction of the James Bay Hydroelectric Project.

4 **1998.** The Aboriginal Healing Foundation, a non-profit corporation to support community healing from Indian Residential Schools, was formed.

5 **1949.** George Arluk (Arlook), Inuit soapstone carver, was born in Keewatin Region, Northwest Territories.

6

7 **1984.** Helen Kalvak, Copper Inuit artist, died at Holman, Northwest Territories. ▶

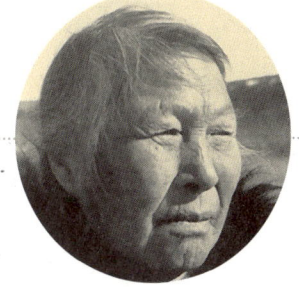

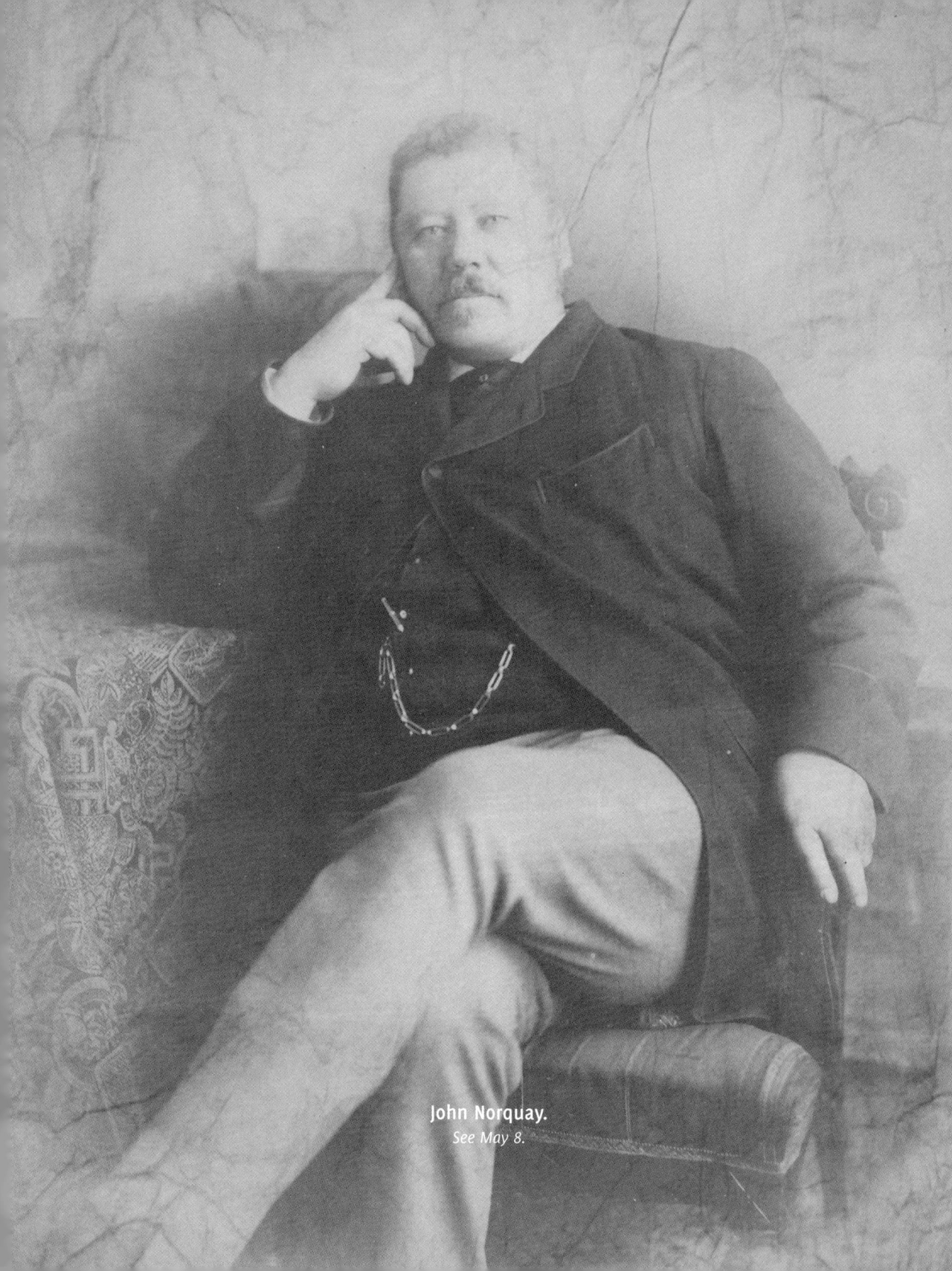

John Norquay.
See May 8.

MAY

8 **1841.** John Norquay was born in what is now Manitoba. He went on to become Manitoba's first Premier of Métis heritage.

9 **1885.** Beginning of the three-day Riel Resistance battle at Batoche. The Steamer *Northcote* is pictured here running the gauntlet during the conflict. ▶

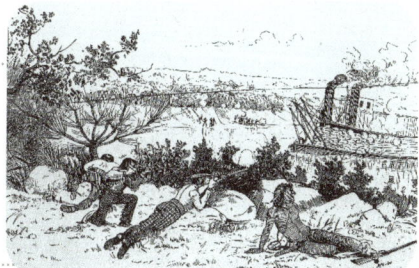

10

11 **1978.** Joe B. Marshall, Mi'kmaw, established a symbolic tollbooth near Eskasoni to protest the Government of Nova Scotia's failure to upgrade highways.

12 **1988.** Josephine Peck, Mi'kmaw from Wagmatcook First Nation, was the first graduate from the Mi'kmaq Bachelor of Social Work program at Dalhousie University; she received her degree at the Dalhousie Convocation Ceremonies held on this day.

13 **2008.** Claudette Dumont-Smith and Jane Morley joined the Truth and Reconciliation Commission as commissioners.

14 **1998.** The Saskatchewan Court of Appeal identified in the *Grumbo* case the need to determine whether Métis had Aboriginal harvesting rights prior to the Natural Resources Transfer Act of 1930.

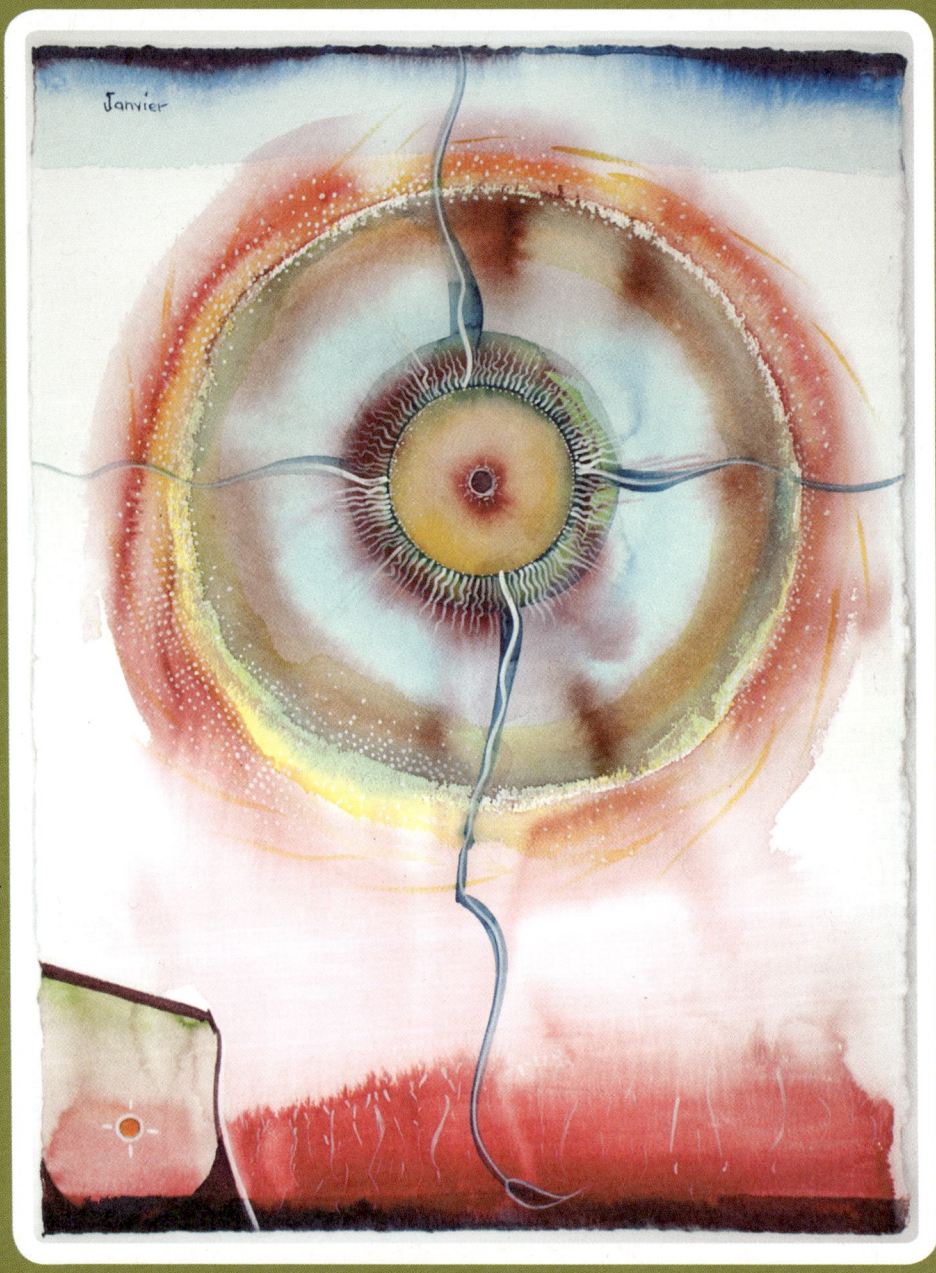

Alex Janvier, *Banff Sunlight on Mountains*.
Watercolour on paper, 30 x 23 inches, 2010.

MAY

15 — **1885.** Louis Riel surrendered to Dominion forces.

16 — **2001.** The last episode of "Dead Dog Café" was performed live at Globe Theatre, Regina, Saskatchewan.

17 — **2001.** Chief Misel Joe of Miawpukek First Nation in Newfoundland and Labrador was appointed to the National Aboriginal Economic Development Board.

18 — **1996.** Ron Irwin, Minister of Indian and Northern Affairs, told Quebec Cree that they could remain part of Canada if Quebec separated.

19 — **1906.** Gabriel Dumont died of a heart attack at home in Bellevue, Saskatchewan.

20 — **1975.** Tahmoh Penikett, Canadian actor, was born in Whitehorse, Yukon. He is the son of former Yukon premier Tony Penikett and Lulla Sierra Johns, a member of White River First Nation. ▶

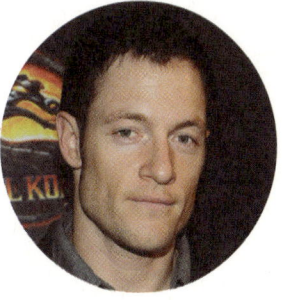

21

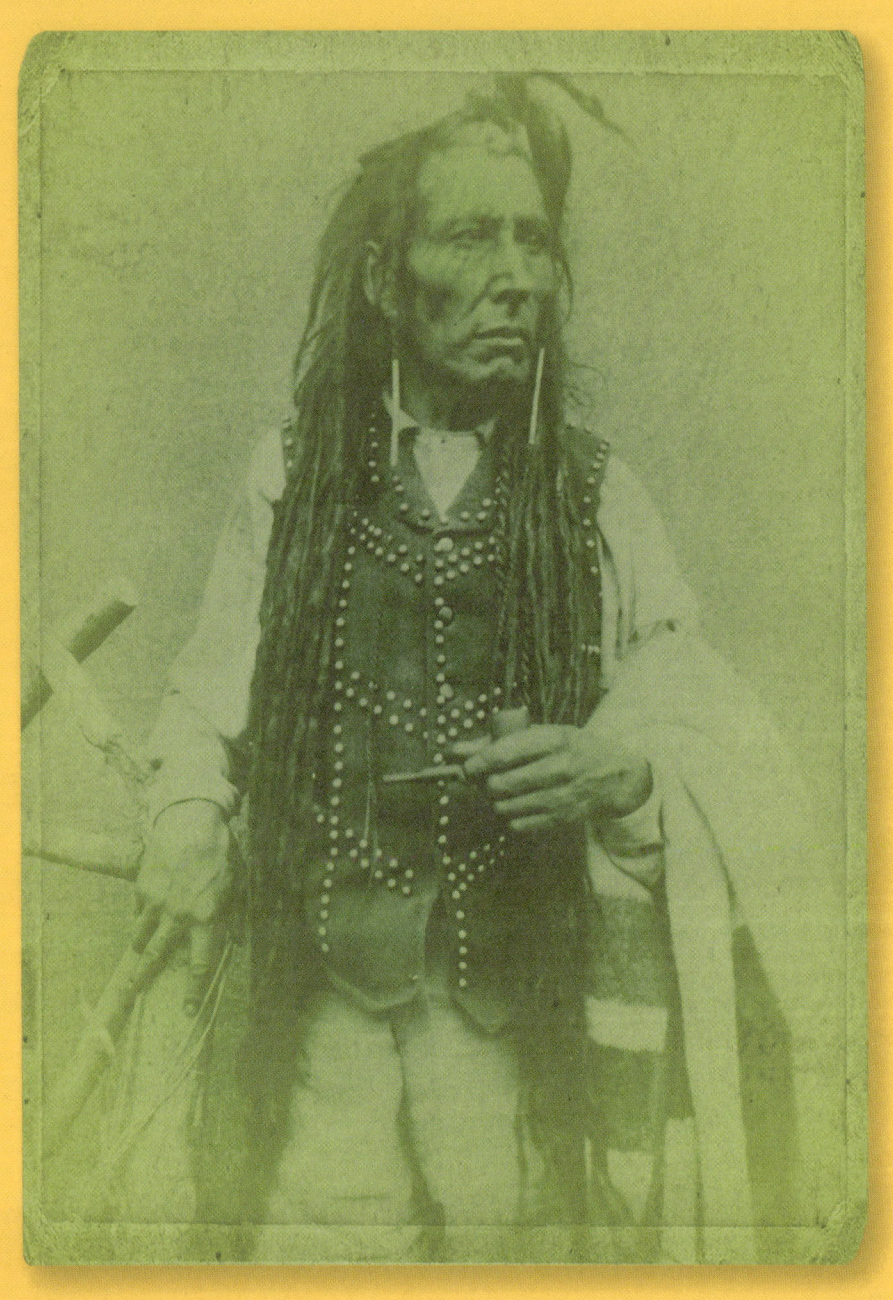

Poundmaker.
See May 26, July 4, and October 13.

MAY

22 **1784.** Mississauga bands agreed to sell land to the British so that Britain's Iroquois allies could relocate to British territory.

23 **1763.** Pontiac, Ottawa Chief, denounced the French as traitors to his cause against British expansion.

24 **1973.** The Government of Canada agreed in principle to the National Indian Brotherhood policy statement asking for "Indian Control of Indian Education."

25 **1959.** George Koneak, Inuit, asked the Government of Canada's Eskimo Affairs Committee to help the Inuit. Left to right: George Koneak, Fort Chimo, Que.; Shinuktuk, Rankin Inlet, N.W.T.; John G. Diefenbaker, Prince Albert, Sask.; Jean Ayaruark, Rankin Inlet, N.W.T.; Abraham Ogpik, Aklavik, N.W.T. ▼

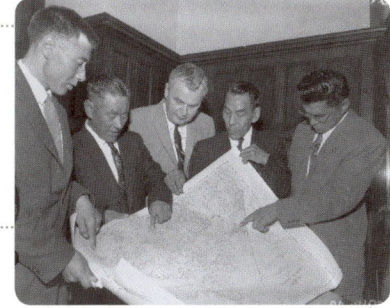

26 **1885.** Pîhtokahânapiwiyin (Plains Cree Chief Poundmaker) surrendered to Major-General Middleton at Battleford, North-West Territories.

27 **2005.** The Manitoba Court of Queen's Bench set April 3, 2006, as the date for the presentation of evidence in the Manitoba Métis Federation and Métis National Council lawsuit against the Governments of Manitoba and Canada.

28

Almighty Voice

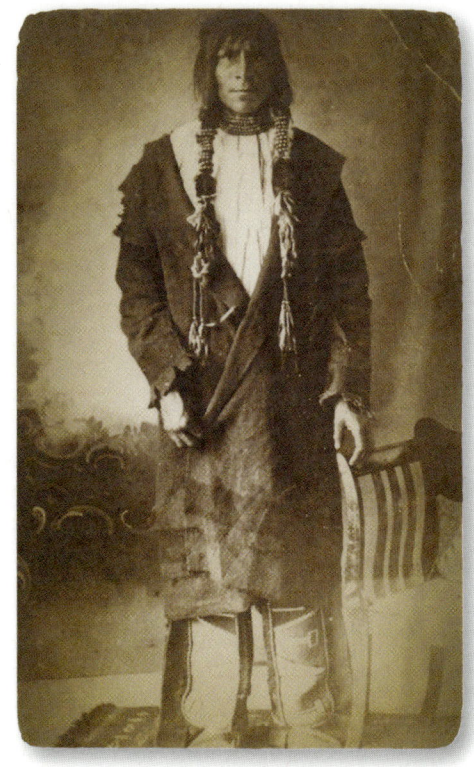

Almighty Voice was born in 1875 near Duck Lake in what is now Saskatchewan. He grew up on the One Arrow Reserve, where he heard stories of his grandfather One Arrow, who had resisted taking up his reserve until 1879. On October 22, 1895, Almighty Voice was arrested by the North-West Mounted Police (NWMP) after being accused of slaughtering a government cow. While he was being transferred to the jail at Duck Lake, one of his arresting officers is said to have joked that the penalty for killing a government cow was hanging. Almighty Voice seemed to have taken the joke seriously: he escaped from jail that night, and fled to his mother's home on the reserve. Initial attempts to capture him were not successful. On October 29, 1895, NWMP officer Colebrook caught up with him near Kinistino, and in the attempted arrest was shot and killed by Almighty Voice. By April 1896 there was a $500 bounty on Almighty Voice; however, he avoided the authorities until May 1897. On May 27, 1897, it was reported that Almighty Voice and two companions had shot and wounded a local Métis scout near Duck Lake. The NWMP under Inspector Allan came across Almighty Voice at the Minichinas Hills, a few miles from the One Arrow Reserve. There was an exchange of gunfire, and Allan and another officer were seriously wounded. Another force made up of both civilians and NWMP officers attempted to rush the three men, but again they were turned away by gunfire. On May 30, after heavy gunfire including rounds from a nine-pound field gun, Almighty Voice, his brother-in-law Topean and his cousin Little Saulteaux were all found dead. (ROB NESTOR)

MAY

29 **1897.** Almighty Voice was killed by North-West Mounted Police officers after he escaped from custody.

30 **2005.** The Government of Canada and the Assembly of First Nations agreed on a new approach to reconciliation.

31 **1916.** Walter Dieter, founding chief of the National Indian Brotherhood, was born on the Peepeekisis Reserve near Balcarres, Saskatchewan.

"No young man can dance forever listening to another man's words."

—MISTAHI-MASKWA (BIG BEAR)

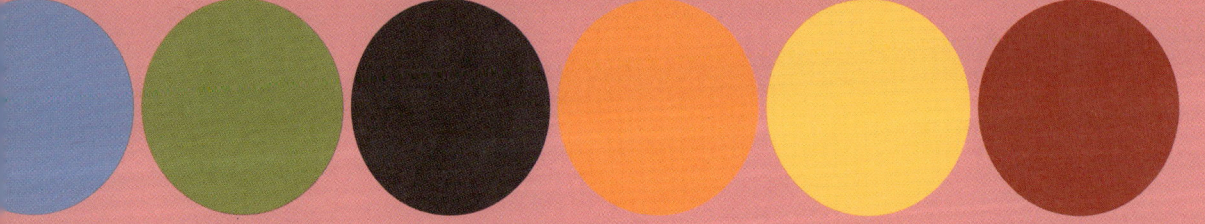

- **1800–1810:** Métis in York Factory invented the York boat, which could hold up to six tons of cargo. The York boat was critical in traversing larger bodies of water during the fur trade.

- **1813** (June 22): First Nations guided Laura Secord to a British camp in order to warn them of an impending attack by the United States during the War of 1812.

- **1818:** Métis physician and surgeon John Bunn was the first native-born doctor to practice medicine in the Red River Settlement.

- **1996** (June 21): Canadians celebrated National Aboriginal Day for the first time.

- **2011:** The Métis now number approximately 350,000–400,000 individuals across Canada, and account for over 25% of the total Aboriginal population in this country.

june

paskawihowipism
(NORTHERN MICHIF)

"Egg-Hatching Moon"

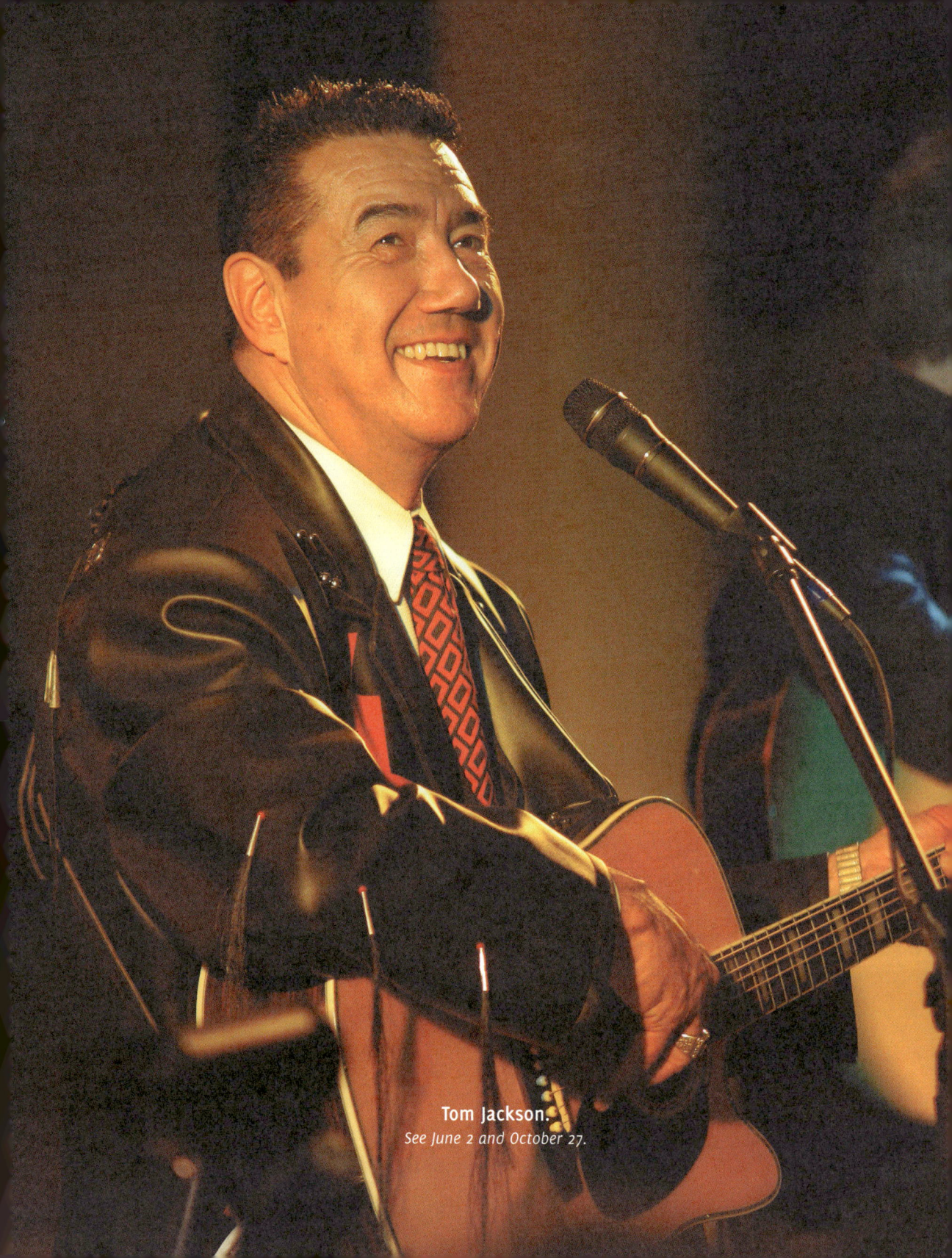

Tom Jackson.
See June 2 and October 27.

JUNE

1 — **1970.** At an interprovincial conference on education in Saskatoon the Saskatchewan Department of Education argued that there was a need for Aboriginal content in K–12 schools.

2 — **1999.** Tom Jackson, Cree singer, actor, and humanitarian, was granted an honourary doctorate by the University of Victoria.

3 — **1985.** The Government of Alberta passed a motion to award fee simple or unlimited title to the eight Alberta Métis Settlements and devolved authority over governance of the lands to the Federation of Alberta Métis Settlements.

4 — **1967.** Michael Greyeyes, Plains Cree actor, choreographer and director, was born at the Muskeg Lake Cree Nation in Saskatchewan. ▶

5 — **1984.** The Inuvialuit Western Arctic Claim was signed.

6 — **2006.** The Federal Standing Committee on Aboriginal Affairs recommended adoption of the draft United Nations Declaration on the Rights of Indigenous Peoples.

7 — **1997.** Daniel N. Paul, Mi'kmaw, received an honourary doctorate from Université Sainte-Anne in Pointe-de-l'Église, Nova Scotia, and delivered the Convocation Address.

Canada Apologizes

EXCERPTS OF PRIME MINISTER HARPER'S STATEMENT OF APOLOGY TO FORMER STUDENTS OF INDIAN RESIDENTIAL SCHOOLS, DELIVERED IN THE HOUSE OF COMMONS ON BEHALF OF THE GOVERNMENT OF CANADA, JUNE 11, 2008.

Mr. Speaker, I stand before you today to offer an apology to former students of Indian residential schools. ... Two primary objectives of the residential schools system were to remove and isolate children from the influence of their homes, families, traditions and cultures, and to assimilate them into the dominant culture. These objectives were based on the assumption aboriginal cultures and spiritual beliefs were inferior and unequal. ... Today, we recognize that this policy of assimilation was wrong, has caused great harm, and has no place in our country. ... The government of Canada built an educational system in which very young children were often forcibly removed from their homes, often taken far from their communities. Many were inadequately fed, clothed and housed. All were deprived of the care and nurturing of their parents, grandparents and communities. First Nations, Inuit and Métis languages and cultural practices were prohibited in these schools. ...Tragically, some of these children died while attending residential schools and others never returned home. The government now recognizes that the consequences of the Indian residential schools policy were profoundly negative and that this policy has had a lasting and damaging impact on aboriginal culture, heritage and language. ... It has taken extraordinary courage for the thousands of survivors that have come forward to speak publicly about the abuse they suffered. ... Therefore, on behalf of the government of Canada and all Canadians, I stand before you ... to apologize to aboriginal peoples for Canada's role in the Indian residential schools system. ... The burden of this experience has been on your shoulders for far too long. ...

THE FULL TEXT CAN BE FOUND ON ABORIGINAL AFFAIRS AND NORTHERN DEVELOPMENT CANADA'S WEBSITE.

> "We recognize that this policy of assimilation was wrong."

JUNE

8   **1931.** Walter Harris, Tsimshian artist and carver, was born at Kispiox, British Columbia. ▶

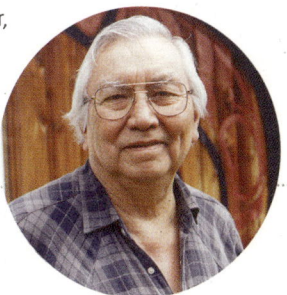

9

10

11   **2008.** Prime Minister Stephen Harper apologized to survivors of Indian Residential Schools.

12   **1953.** Gary Farmer, Cayuga actor, was born in Ohsweken, Ontario. ▶

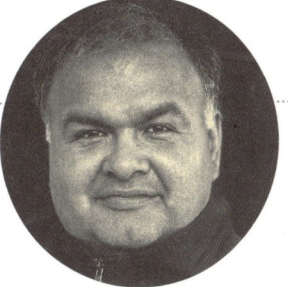

13   **1977.** Indigenous peoples from Canada, Alaska, and Greenland convened the first Inuit Circumpolar Conference in Barrows, Alaska.

14   **1985.** 150 Dene and Métis around Wollaston Lake, Saskatchewan, blocked access to uranium mines that were contaminating fish and wildlife and offering the local Aboriginals little employment.

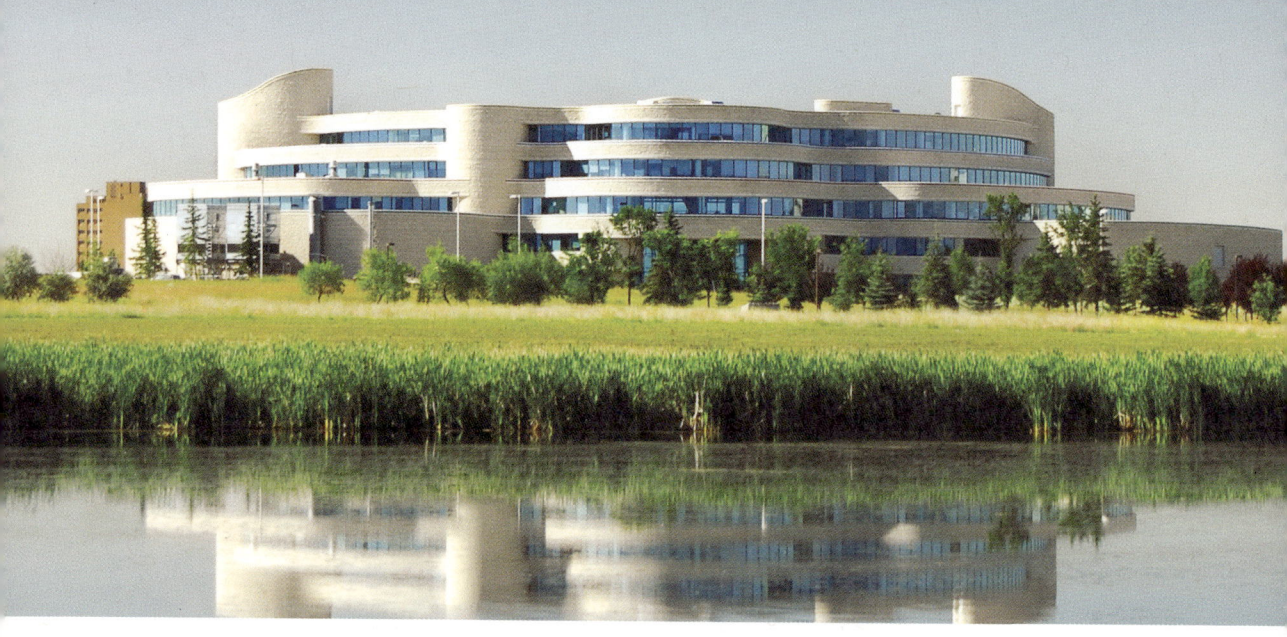

The First Nations University of Canada (FNUC)

The First Nations University of Canada is a post-secondary institution for both First Nations and non-First Nations students. Founded in 1976 as the Saskatchewan Indian Federated College, the First Nations University of Canada has been independently administered since its inception but began in federated partnership with the University of Regina. Its main campus is at the University of Regina in Regina—there are two other campuses in Saskatoon and Prince Albert, Saskatchewan. The university offers programs, degrees, and classes in a culturally supportive environment, providing courses in Indigenous studies, literature, linguistics, First Nations languages, First Nations education, administration, social work, and First Nations fine arts among its programs. However, the university has faced challenges: in 2007 it was suspected of being politically interfered with by the Federation of Saskatchewan Indian Nations (FSIN) and was temporarily placed on probation by the Association of Universities and Colleges of Canada, and in 2010 the university announced plans to fiscally restructure after financial trouble was reported. Despite these setbacks, however, the University has become the pre-eminent institution for those scholars seeking First Nations perspectives on modern, western knowledge.

(JAMES OSTIME)

JUNE

15

16 1816. The Battle of Seven Oaks was fought near Red River. The battle is credited by historians as the crucible of Métis identity formation in the West. ▶

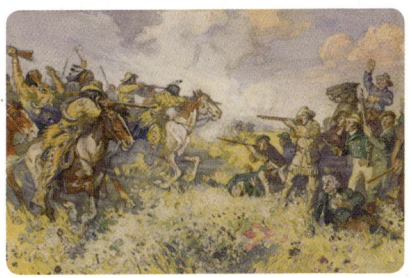

17 1984. Marie Battiste, Mi'kmaw educator from Potlo'tek First Nations of Unama'kik, Nova Scotia, received her Ed.D. from Stanford University. She went on to develop a bilingual Mi'kmaq-English program for the Chapel Island School and become a Professor of Education in the Department of Educational Foundations, College of Education, University of Saskatchewan.

18 1991. The first conference of Indian Residential School survivors was held in Vancouver.

19 1974. Non-status First Nations in Newfoundland and Labrador held their first general assembly.

20 1969. The Government of Canada approved policy to disestablish the Department of Indian Affairs and Northern Development.

21 2003. The First Nations University of Canada officially opened, on National Aboriginal Day.

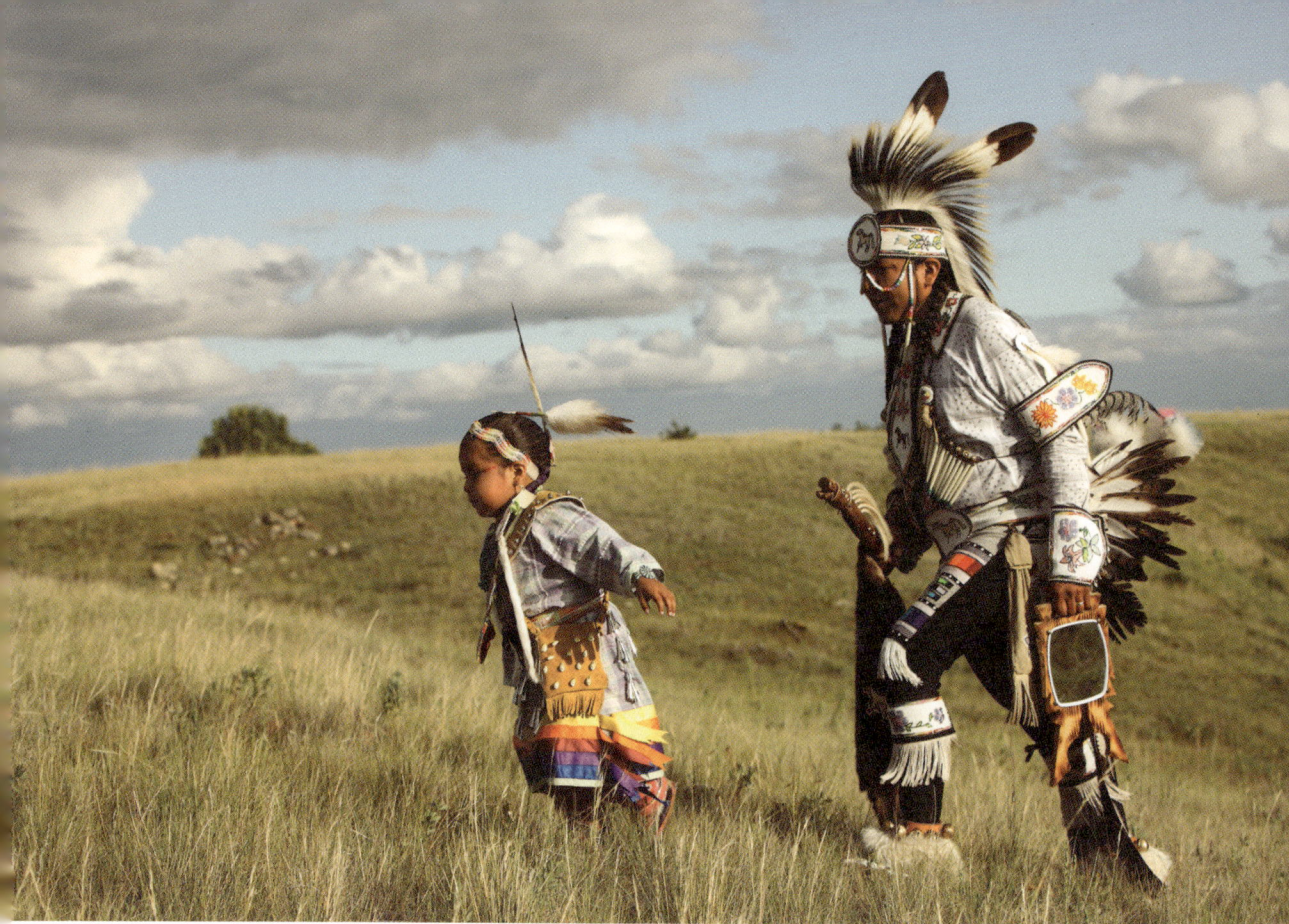

Wanuskewin

Wanuskewin Heritage Park is a non-profit interpretative centre, a major tourist attraction, and an internationally renowned historical monument for northern Plains First Nations. The area itself, along the west bank of the South Saskatchewan River and north of the city of Saskatoon, has been used by the northern Plains First Nations (among them the Plains Cree, the Plains Ojibwe, the Dakota Sioux, and Assiniboine) for more than 6,000 years to hunt, gather, and find shelter. Now the heritage park, designated a historical site in 1986 by the Canadian government, and opened as a national park in 1992, is home to many artifacts, camp sites, bison kill sites, walking trails, and an arrangement of boulders comprising a medicine wheel. The area was first scientifically investigated in the 1930s and is now part of an archaeological research program developed by the University of Saskatchewan. (JAMES OSTIME)

JUNE

22 — **1952.** Graham Greene, acclaimed Oneida film and television actor, was born on the Six Nations Reserve in Ontario. ▶

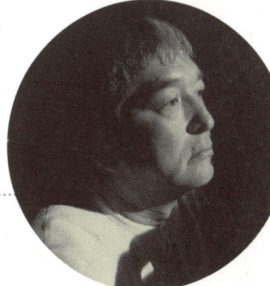

23 — **1980.** The Mi'kmaq Arts and Crafts Society named Peter Poulette, Mi'kmaw from Eskasoni First Nation in Nova Scotia, Craftsman of the Year.

24 — **1870.** The Manitoba Act was passed by the Provisional Government at the Red River Settlement.

25 — **1968.** Leonard Marchand became the first person of First Nation ancestry to be elected as a Member of Parliament.

26 — **1984.** Richard Cardinal, Métis from Fort Chipewyan, Alberta, committed suicide on his foster parents' farm outside of Edmonton. Cardinal's suicide resulted in an investigation of the provincial Department of Social Services' protocols and practices concerning First Nations and Métis children in care in the province.

27 — **1992.** Wanuskewin Heritage Park opened near Saskatoon, Saskatchewan. ▶

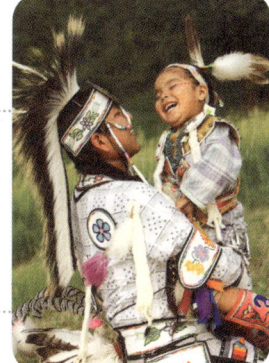

28 — **1985.** Bill C-31 became law, enabling Aboriginal women who lost their First Nations status through marriage to non-Status First Nations men to apply to have their Indian Status reinstated under the Indian Act. However, the Bill provided status only to those women who lost it and to the next generation of descendants.

The Métis Sash

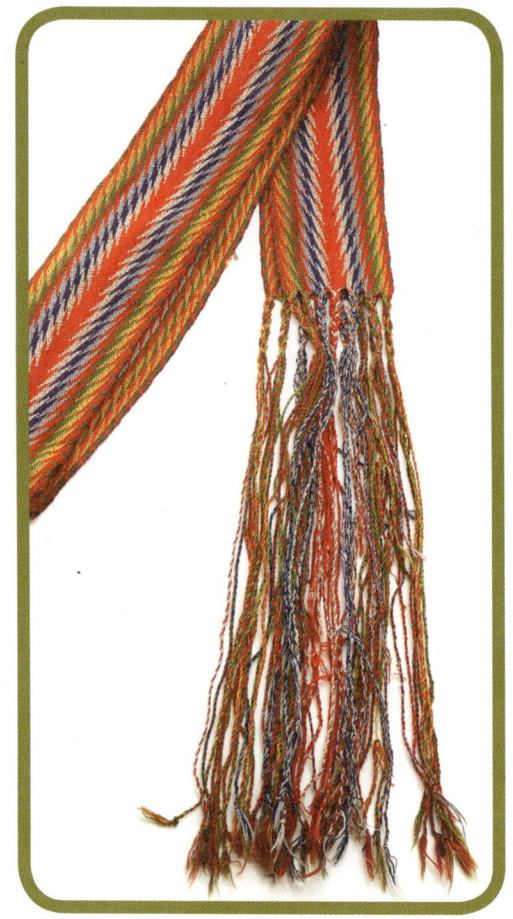

The ceinture fléchée, or Assomption sash, pictured here, was brought to Alberta in the 1880s by Duncan Campbell, who had moved west from St. Hilaire, Quebec. It was likely woven by Campbell's mother, or a local woman from the St. Hilaire community.

Since the seventeenth century, the most well-known piece of Métis iconography is the ceinture fléchée, also known as the Métis sash and the Assomption sash. The latter name is given because the sash was originally sewn in L'Assomption, Quebec. The sash was originally a practical and functional piece of clothing for the Métis voyageurs who wore it. Woven by hand out of wool, the sash was used as a key holder, washcloth, towel, saddle blanket and, because of its fringed edges, an emergency sewing kit—a most useful article of clothing indeed to these paddlers who were so vital to the fur trade. By the early nineteenth century, the sash had become strongly identified with the Métis and it began to take on the great cultural significance that it carries today. Sashes were created using distinct colours and patterns that identified the home community of the Métis wearer. Today, the colours used in the sashes also reflect Métis identity: blue and white has come to symbolize the Métis Nation flag; green is associated with fertility and growth; yellow signifies prosperity; and red and white represent the Métis hunting flag. (JAMES OSTIME)

JUNE

29   **2006.** The United Nations Human Rights Council adopted the draft Declaration on the Rights of Indigenous Peoples.

30   **1982.** The Federation of Métis Settlements released their constitutional position paper entitled "Métisism," a document that "asserted the belief of [Métis] settlement residents that they were the owners of their land and resources." In "Métisism" the Federation of Métis Settlements recommended Métis representation in Alberta's legislature through an elected constituency seat, a voting position on the Northlands School Division Board, protection of the Michif language in the Alberta School Act's minority language education framework, and consensus-style negotiations with the Government of Alberta.

"Only when the last tree has died
and the last river has been poisoned
and the last fish has been caught
will we realize
we cannot eat money."

—CREE INDIAN PROVERB

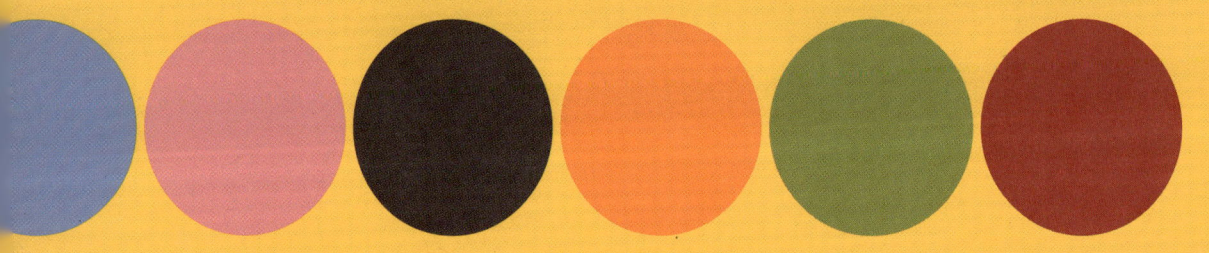

- **1862–1863 and 1876–1877:** Sioux bands sought refuge in Canada following their clashes with the United States Army. They continue to be considered as refugees by the Canadian government, and as such have not been signatories to treaties, unlike all other Plains First Nations.

- **1870** (July 15): The Manitoba Act took effect, granting the Métis 1.4 million acres of land. Subsequently, many Métis were coerced out of their land and moved west into what is now Saskatchewan.

- **1970** (July/August): The first issue of *New Breed Magazine* was published by the Métis Society of Saskatchewan.

- **2009** (July 23): Shawn A-in-chut Atleo, of the Ahousaht First Nation on Vancouver Island, was elected chief of the Assembly of First Nations.

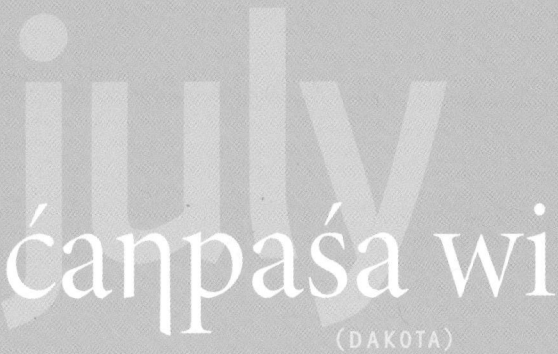

july
ćanpaśa wi
(DAKOTA)

"Red Chokecherries Moon"

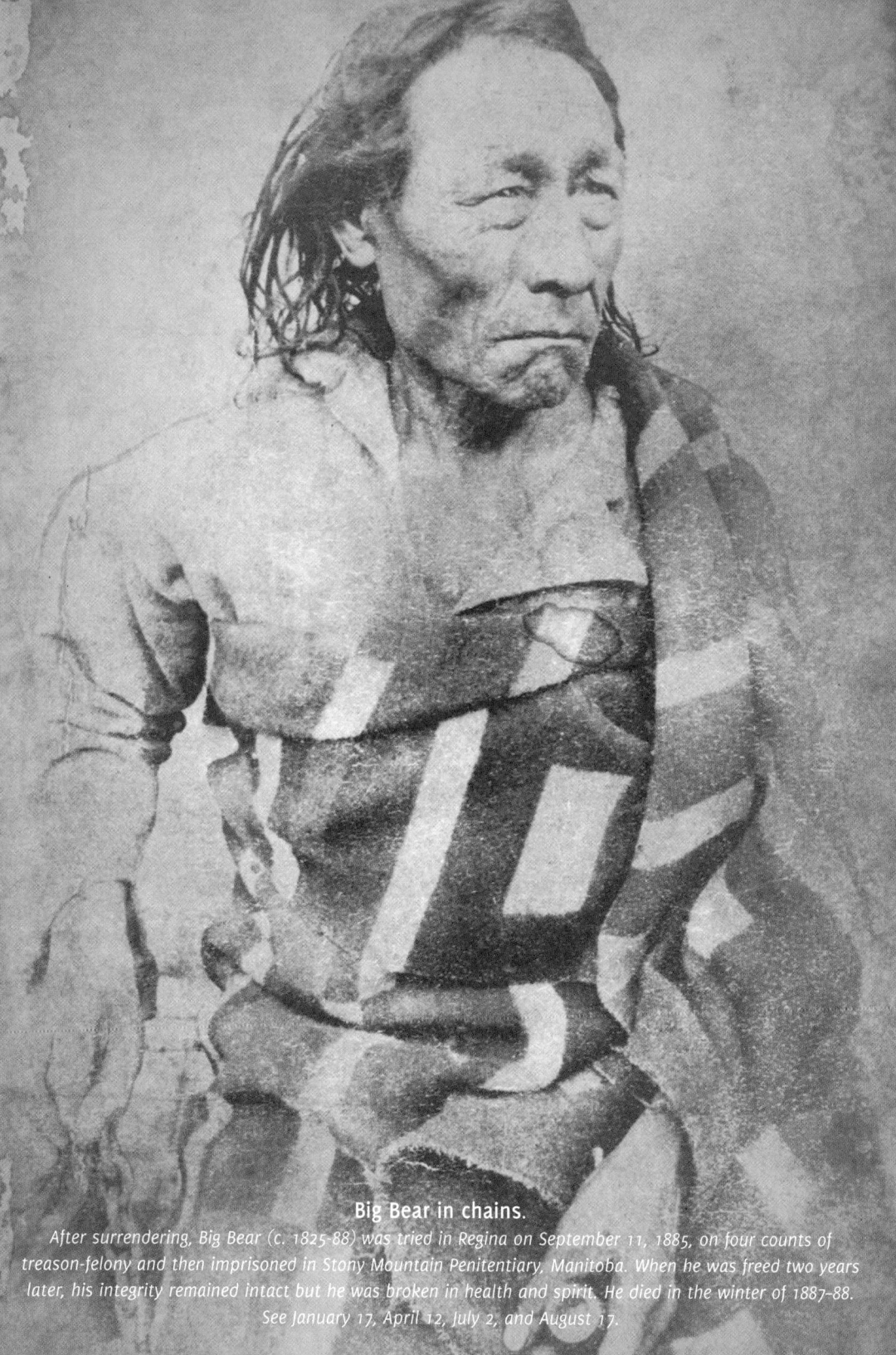

Big Bear in chains.
After surrendering, Big Bear (c. 1825-88) was tried in Regina on September 11, 1885, on four counts of treason-felony and then imprisoned in Stony Mountain Penitentiary, Manitoba. When he was freed two years later, his integrity remained intact but he was broken in health and spirit. He died in the winter of 1887–88. See January 17, April 12, July 2, and August 17.

JULY

1   **1967.** David Knight, former chief of the Federation of Saskatchewan Indian Nations, received a Centennial Medal.

2   **1885.** Big Bear surrendered near Fort Carlton.

3   **1980.** Native Council of Canada President Harry Daniels and his board of directors attended the Liberal Party policy convention to lobby for "full and equal Aboriginal participation in the constitutional review process."

4   **1886.** Pîhtokahânapiwiyin (Plains Cree Chief Poundmaker) died at Blackfoot Crossing, Alberta.

5   **1998.** Haida artist Bill Reid's ashes were interred at his ancestral village of Ttanuu, Haida Gwaii, British Columbia.

6   **1930.** George Armstrong, one of Canada's first professional Aboriginal hockey players, was born in Skead, Ontario. ▶

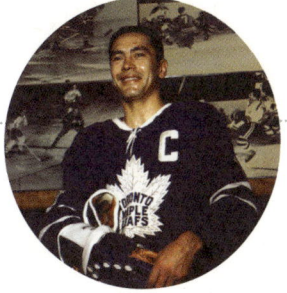

7   **2004.** The Ontario Ministry of Natural Resources and the Métis Nation of Ontario (MNO) entered interim Métis harvesting agreement; the Government of Ontario "agreed to recognize MNO harvester certificates in Métis traditional territories in ON [as had been] identified by the MNO."

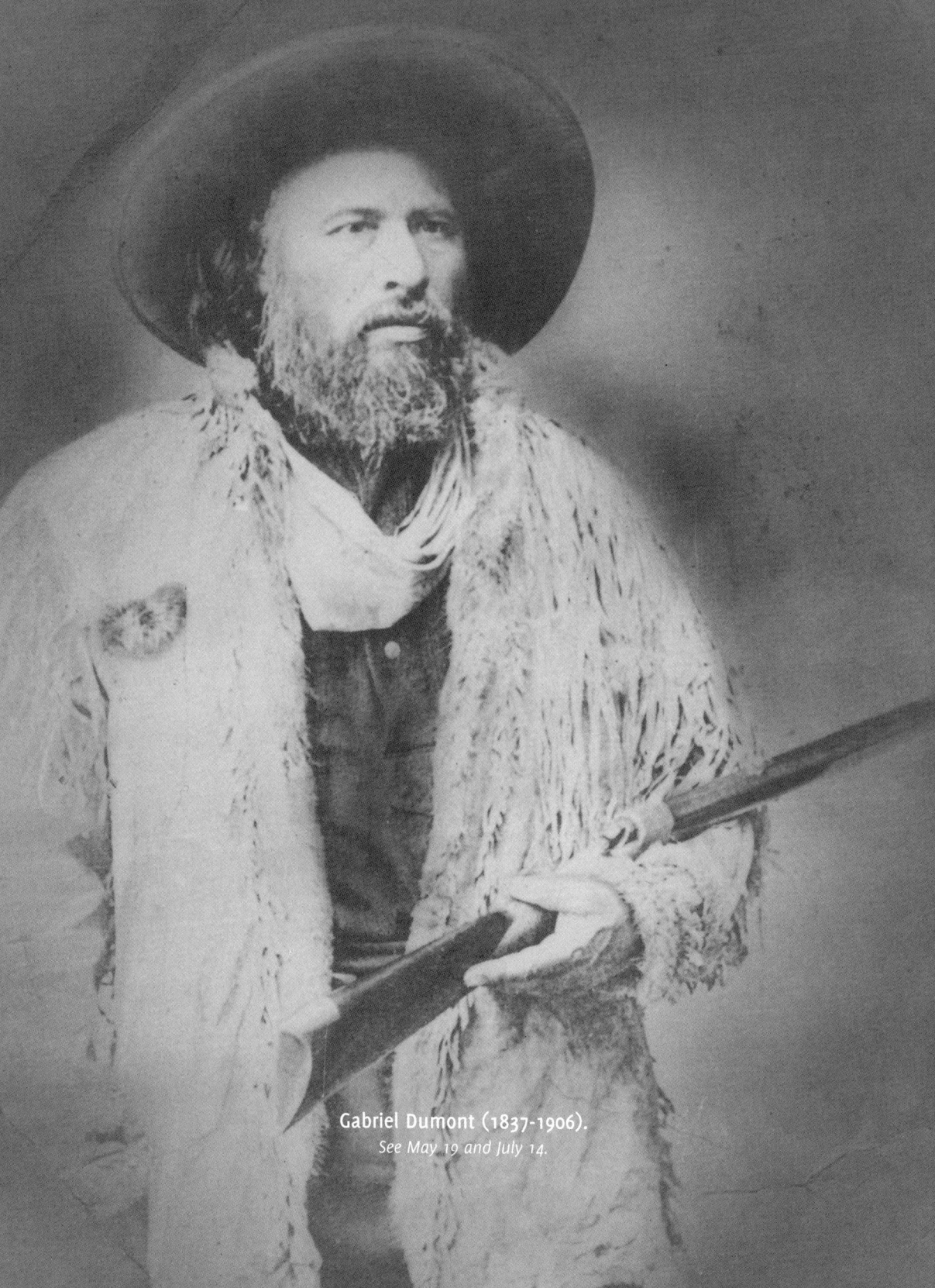

Gabriel Dumont (1837-1906).
See May 19 and July 14.

JULY

8 **1984.** Apitchitchiw, Chief Johnny Bob Smallboy, Cree activist, died at Smallboy Camp, Alberta. Smallboy had been invested as a Member of the Order of Canada in 1980.

9

10

11 **1990.** Police attacked the Mohawk blockade at Oka, resulting in the death of one police officer.

12 **2000.** Matthew Coon Come, James Bay Cree, was elected National Chief of the Assembly of First Nations.

13 **1971.** Charles Labrador was elected the first Chief of Acadia First Nation in Yarmouth, Nova Scotia.

14 **1851.** Gabriel Dumont and 300 Métis defeated Yankton Dakota at the Battle of Grand Coteau in what is now North Dakota.

Bob Boyer

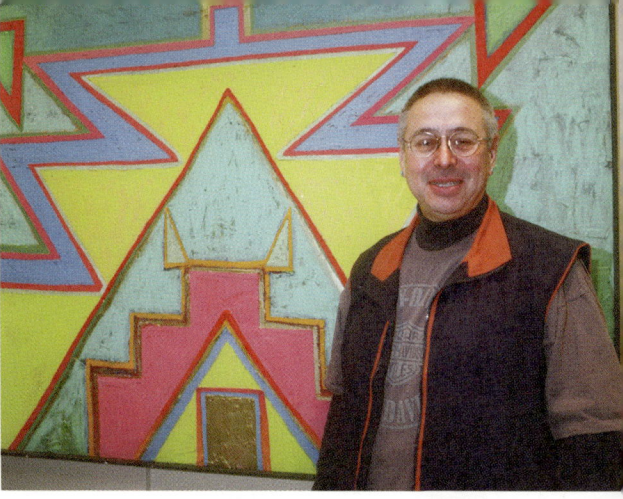

Bob Boyer at Cumberland Gallery in the Saskatchewan Legislative Building, November 7, 2001.

Bob Boyer (1948-2004) was a painter, installation artist, powwow dancer, social activist, educator, author of several art catalogues and reviews, curator of a significant number of art exhibitions, and a national and international exhibitor. Of Métis heritage, he was born on July 20, 1948, in Prince Albert, Saskatchewan. In 1971, he received a B.Ed. (Arts Education) from the University of Regina, and upon returning to Prince Albert began teaching at St. Mary's High School. In 1977, Boyer was hired as program consultant for the Saskatchewan Indian Federated College's (now the First Nations University of Canada) Department of Indian Fine Arts. He was Department Head between 1979 and 1997, and was a highly respected art and art history instructor.

Boyer's career as a professional artist began in 1971 and was recognized as a critical element in the development of contemporary First Nations art. His artistic versatility enabled him to move from one medium and technique to another, incorporating Northern Plains First Nations geometric design to reflect personal experiences, social issues, and spirituality. Boyer was best known for his politically charged "blanket statements," which critically reviewed the effects of non-First Nation influence on First Nations people and land. He painted these accounts on blanket canvasses representing the distribution of Hudson's Bay blankets infected with smallpox, and each piece marks how colonialism impacted the Aboriginal and Métis people. In 1994 Boyer's work underwent a change in direction, and although he continued to use traditional symbols, motifs and icons, his art began to exhibit a place of spiritual calm from which he celebrated First Nations' cultures, peoples and events.

Boyer's artistic influence and teaching have provided direction and understanding to First Nations and non-First Nation students alike for First Nations' art and art history. Bob Boyer died on August 30, 2004. (CHRISTIAN THOMPSON)

JULY

15   **2005.** Judge Kalenith of the Provincial Court of Saskatchewan ruled in favour of a Métis defendant from Meadow Lake charged with violation of provincial fishery regulations. The Judge believed there was sufficient evidence to support an historical rights-bearing Métis community not only in northwest Saskatchewan but in the regions immediately south of the territory.

16

17   **1980.** 28 women MPs announced they would fight for a repeal of the section of the Indian Act that took away status rights from First Nations women upon marriage to non-Status First Nations.

18   **1999.** The canoe *Spirit Wind* and its Mi'kmaw crew arrived at Neil's Harbour, Cape Breton, Nova Scotia, after making a trip from Newfoundland across the Cabot Strait to Nova Scotia, a trip that had not been undertaken by Mi'kmaq for over 100 years.

19   **1964.** Floyd Favel Starr, Cree, playwright and Jasper Friendly Bear on "Dead Dog Café," was born on the Poundmaker Reserve, Saskatchewan.

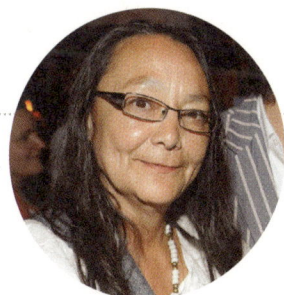

20   **1950.** Acclaimed Cree/Métis actress Tantoo Cardinal was born in Fort McMurray, Alberta. Cardinal was made a member of the Order of Canada in 2009. ▲

1948. Acclaimed Métis artist Bob Boyer was born.

21   **1822.** Henry Budd, first Cree Anglican minister, was baptized at Norway House, Rupert's Land. ▶

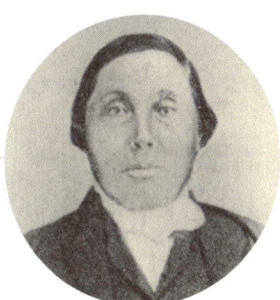

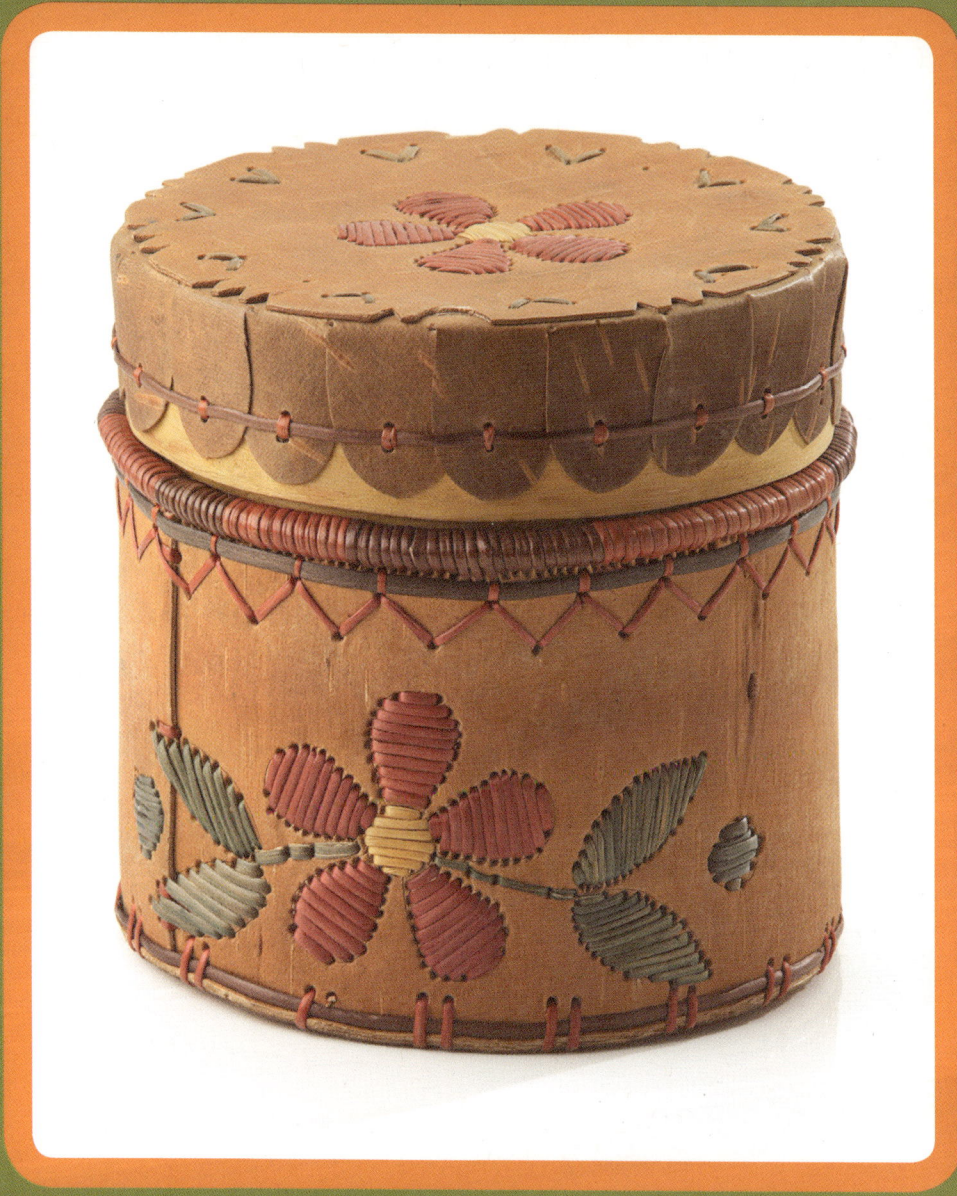

Nehiwyan basket.
c. early 20th century.

JULY

22

23 **1921.** Wilfred Bellegarde, future chief of the Federation of Saskatchewan Indian Nations, was born at the Little Black Bear Reserve.

24 **1944.** Jackson Beardy, Cree, member of the "Indian Group of Seven," was born on the Garden Hill First Nation Reserve, Island Lake, Manitoba. He died on December 7, 1984.

25 **1761.** The terms of a peace agreement between Mi'kmaq, Wuastukwiuk, Passamaquoddy, and the British were formalized at Halifax.

26

27 **1994.** A controversial statue of Louis Riel was removed from the grounds of the Manitoba legislature.

28 **1921.** Chief Julius Salu of the Tetlit Gwich'in signed Treaty 11 in Fort McPherson, Yukon Territory, with the Government of Canada.

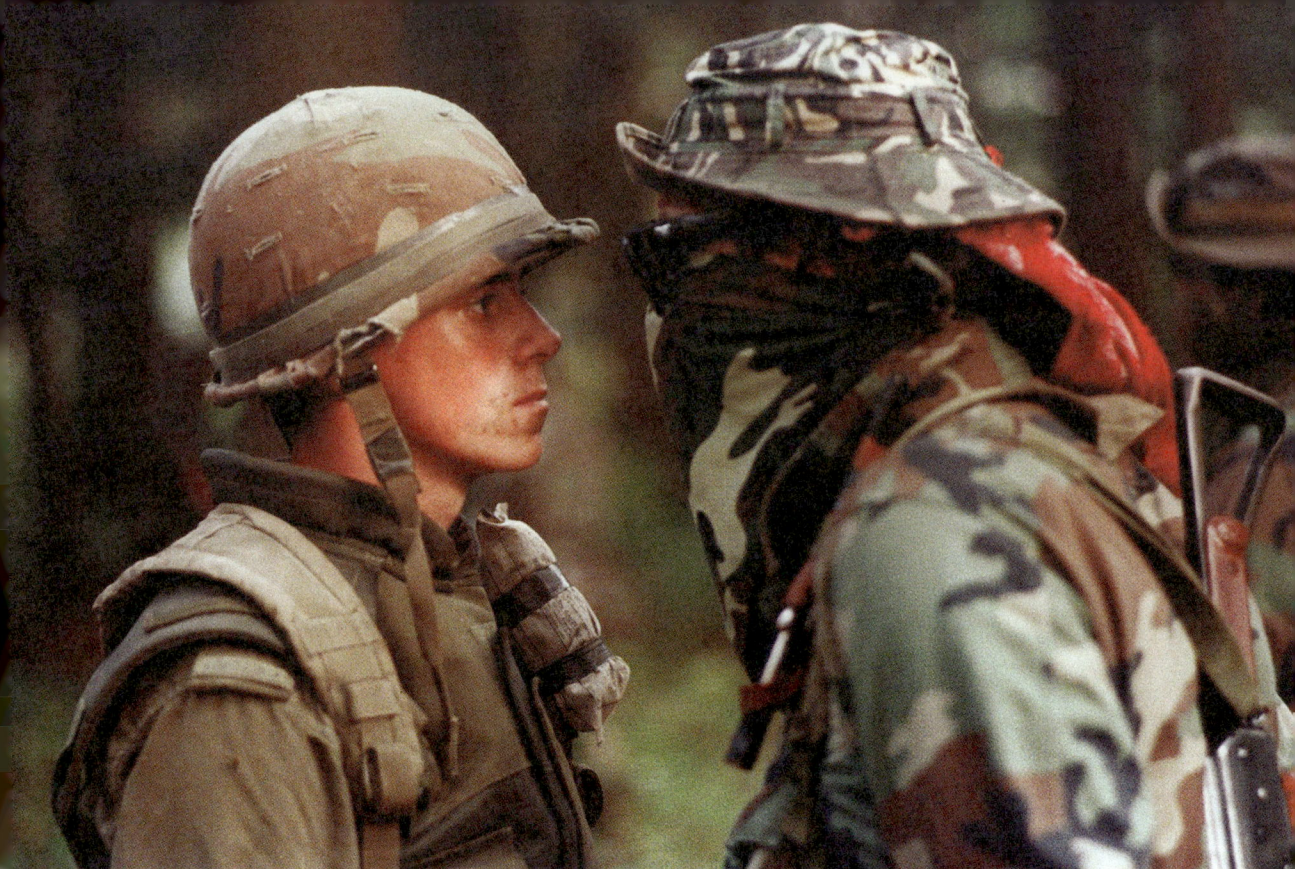

The Oka Crisis

The Oka Crisis began as a land dispute in the summer of 1990 and culminated in a 78-day standoff that left one person dead and damaged relations between the Quebec town of Oka and the nearby Mohawk nation of the Kanesatake. The disputed territory was initially granted in the early 18th century to a Roman Catholic seminary, though the Mohawk maintain that such a grant was illegal. In 1936, the seminary left the land, and the Mohawk of Kanesatake considered it theirs. In 1989, the mayor of Oka, Jean Ouellette, announced plans to build a golf course on this land without consulting the Mohawk community and as a result, in July 1990, members of Kanesatake erected a barricade which rendered the area inaccessible. Ouellette demanded the barrier be removed, and when the Kanesatake failed to comply, sent in the Sûreté du Québec (the Quebec provincial police force). The police attacked the protestors at the

JULY

29 — **1990.** The Assembly of First Nations organized an Oka peace rally to support the Mohawk blockade. Approximately 2,500 people took part.

30 — **1946.** The Co-operative Commonwealth Federation (CCF) held a Métis Convention at the Regina Court House to revive the Métis Society of Saskatchewan.

31

barricade with flash-bang grenades and canisters of tear gas. Shots were fired, and though it is unclear whether the Mohawk protestors or police fired shots first, police officer Marcel Lemay was shot in the face and died. The conflict became national news, and the standoff intensified. First Nations people from across North America travelled to the disputed area and Ouellette sent in the RCMP. The RCMP was instructed not to use force and became quickly overwhelmed by the number of protestors; ten constables were sent to hospital with injuries. Another blockade was erected, this time blocking the Mercier Bridge which connected the Island of Montreal to the suburbs of the South Shore. On August 29, that blockade was taken down after lengthy negotiation and on September 26 the standoff finally came to a close. The Mohawks took their guns, dismantled and burned them, along with tobacco in a ceremonial fire, and walked back to the Kanesatake reservation. Plans for the golf course were cancelled, but relations between the Mohawk and Oka residents and authorities remained strained. (JAMES OSTIME)

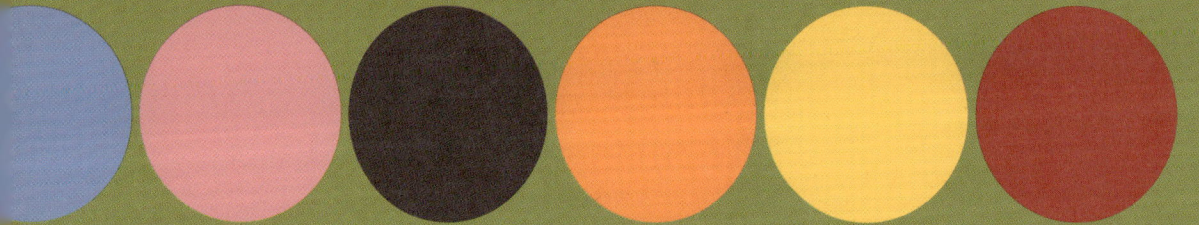

- **1640:** The first known reference to the Ojibwe occurs in the *Jesuit Relations* of that year.

- **1951 (August 1):** Alootook Ipellie, Inuit writer, was born on the north shore of Frobisher Bay, Northwest Territories (now Nunavut).

- **1973:** The Government of Canada accepted the principle of the National Indian Brotherhood policy statement entitled "Indian Control of Indian Education."

- **2003:** The National Residential School Survivors' Society is formed at an informal gathering of Indian Residential School survivors.

august
miini-giizis
(OJIBWE)
"Berry Moon"

The Nisga'a Treaty

The Nisga'a Nation made history in April 2000, when the Nisga'a Final Agreement Act was passed, thereby granting the Nisga'a Treaty, one of only 14 modern-day treaties in Canada, and the first of its kind in British Columbia (B.C.). The majority of the Nisga'a people have resided in the Nass River Valley of northwest B.C. since time immemorial. They speak predominantly English now but teach their traditional language in schools. In recent years, they have revitalized their tradition of carving and erecting totem poles. While they seek to preserve their rich heritage, the Nisga'a have always been politically progressive. They were the first of Canada's First Nations to legally initiate a land claim against the government of Canada (in 1912), after forming the Nisga'a Land Committee in 1890. However, their claim was difficult to pursue, as First Nations people were prohibited by Canadian laws from raising funds for land claims (in 1951 these laws were repealed). The Nisga'a Land Committee became the Nisga'a Tribal Council in 1955, when they again sought the right to govern themselves and claim the land as their own. They went to court in 1969, claiming that, because their land had never been legally surrendered in any way, it remained theirs. These claims of the Nisga'a were dismissed in B.C. courts, so they went to the Supreme Court of Canada, where it was conceded that while they had a right to their land, no agreement was reached as to how these rights were to be determined or evaluated. After more than 25 years in legal battles, an agreement in principle (AIP) was signed in 1996 by the Nisga'a people and representatives from provincial and federal governments. This AIP outlined what became the Nisga'a Treaty, passed in April 2000. The Nisga'a have become a self-governing people recognized by Canadian law, with their own health board, school district, and post-secondary institution. Though the policies and practices of this government must work in concert with provincial and federal laws, it is this important distinction of self-governance through the Nisga'a Treaty that is the Nisga'a Nation's significant and historic achievement.

(JAMES OSTIME)

AUGUST

1 **1976.** Alasua Amittuq Davidialuk, Inuit artist, died during an emergency evacuation flight near Povungnituk.

2

3 **1871.** Seven First Nations signed Treaty 1 with the Government of Canada at Lower Fort Garry, Manitoba.

4 **1998.** The Nisga'a Tribal Council signed the first treaty in British Columbia since the province joined Confederation in 1871.

5

6 **2009.** Mi'kmaw Donald Marshall, Jr. died. Marshall was wrongfully convicted of murder in 1971 and was imprisoned for 11 years.

7 **1907.** Leaders at Fishing Lake First Nation in Saskatchewan signed a separation agreement from Nut Lake First Nation.

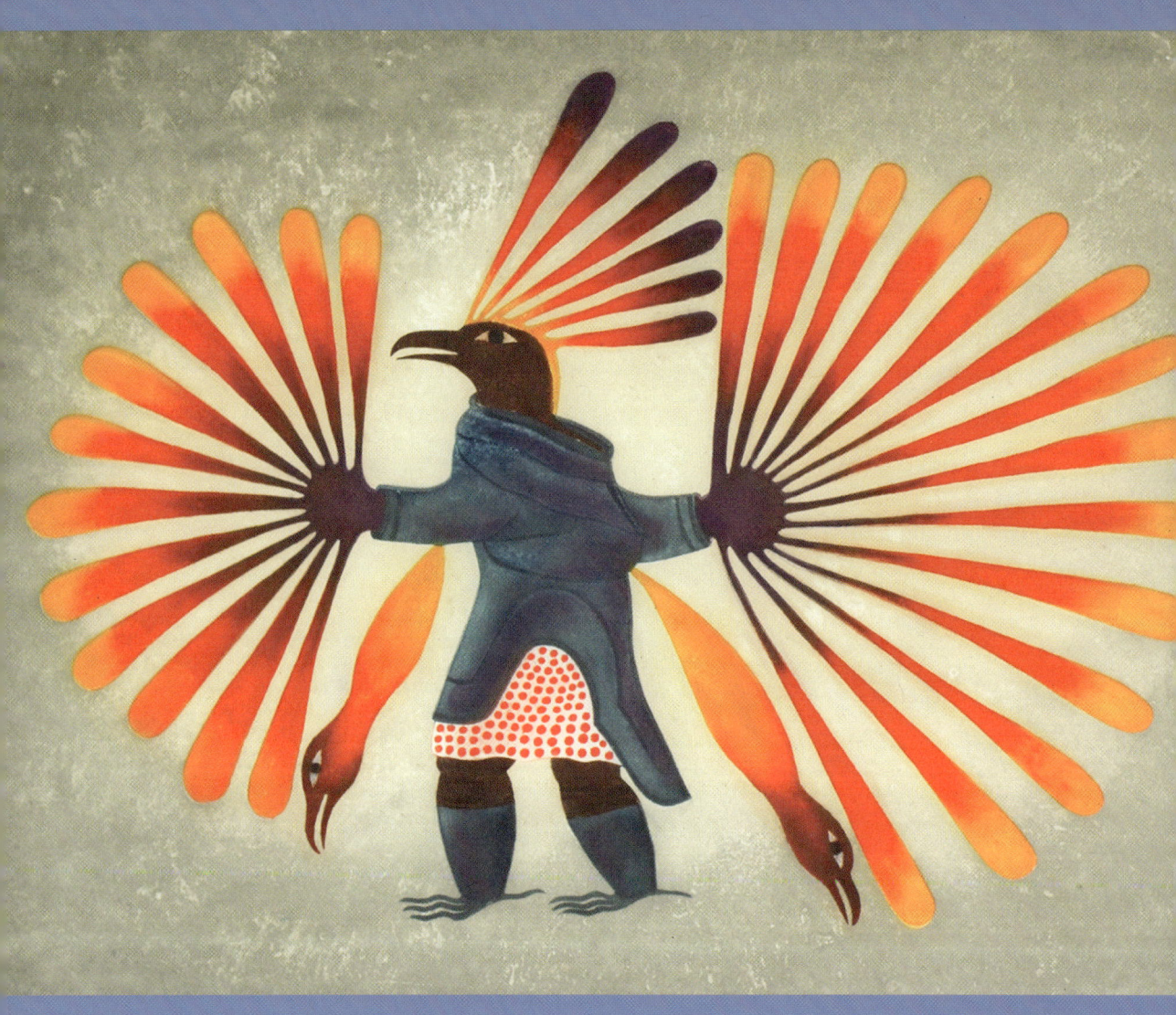

Kenojuak Ashevak, *Spirit of the Sun.*
Print media, 25.5 x 32 inches, 1998.
See October 3 and the page facing the week of October 15-21.

AUGUST

8 — **1993.** Protestors blocked Kennedy Lake Bridge on Vancouver Island in an attempt to prevent loggers from entering Clayoquot Sound.

9 — International Day of the World's Indigenous People.

10 — **1850.** The first legal definition of "Indian" established by the Government of Britain for Canada.

11 — **1984.** Alwyn Morris, Mohawk, won two medals in pairs kayaking (gold and bronze) at the 1984 Olympic games in Los Angeles.

12 —

13 — **1997.** Rachel Mary Marshall, the first woman in Atlantic Canada to be elected Chief of a band council, died at age 87. Marshall was elected the Chief of Millbrook First Nation near Truro, Nova Scotia, in 1969.

14 —

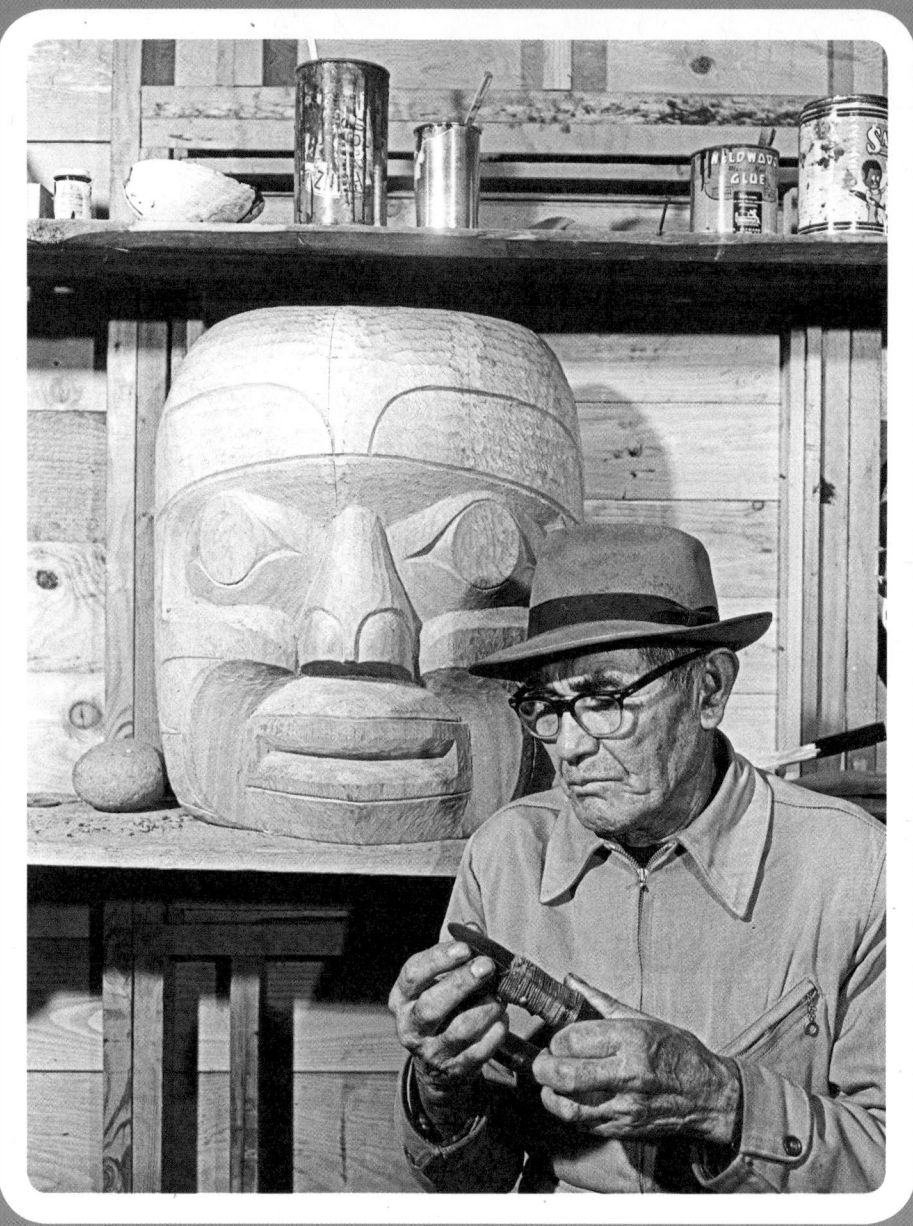

Kwakuitl Chief Mungo Martin, 1954.
The chief is shown here with a mask carved for photographer George Hunter.
See August 16.

AUGUST

15
1969. The Educational Council, Government of Saskatchewan, approved the first Native Studies high school course in Saskatchewan for E. D. Feehan High School in Saskatoon. The course was entitled "History and Culture of Indian People."

16
1962. Mungo Martin, Kwakwaka'wakw carver, singer, painter, and songwriter, died in Victoria, British Columbia.

17
1884. Big Bear met Louis Riel at Duck Lake to discuss First Nations and Métis joining in resistance against Canada.

18
1971. The Inuit Tapirisat of Canada was formed as a national alliance of Inuit organizations. Tagak Curley was elected as the first President.

19
1928. Qaqaq Ashoona, Inuit sculptor, was born in the Northwest Territories.

20
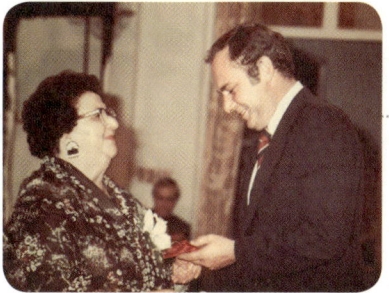

21
1996. Mary Two-Axe Early, the first Aboriginal woman to regain status under Bill C-31, died.

1979: Governor General Edward Schreyer presents Mary Two-Axe Early with the Governor General's Award in Commemoration of the Persons Case. The award is given to outstanding Canadian women. ▲

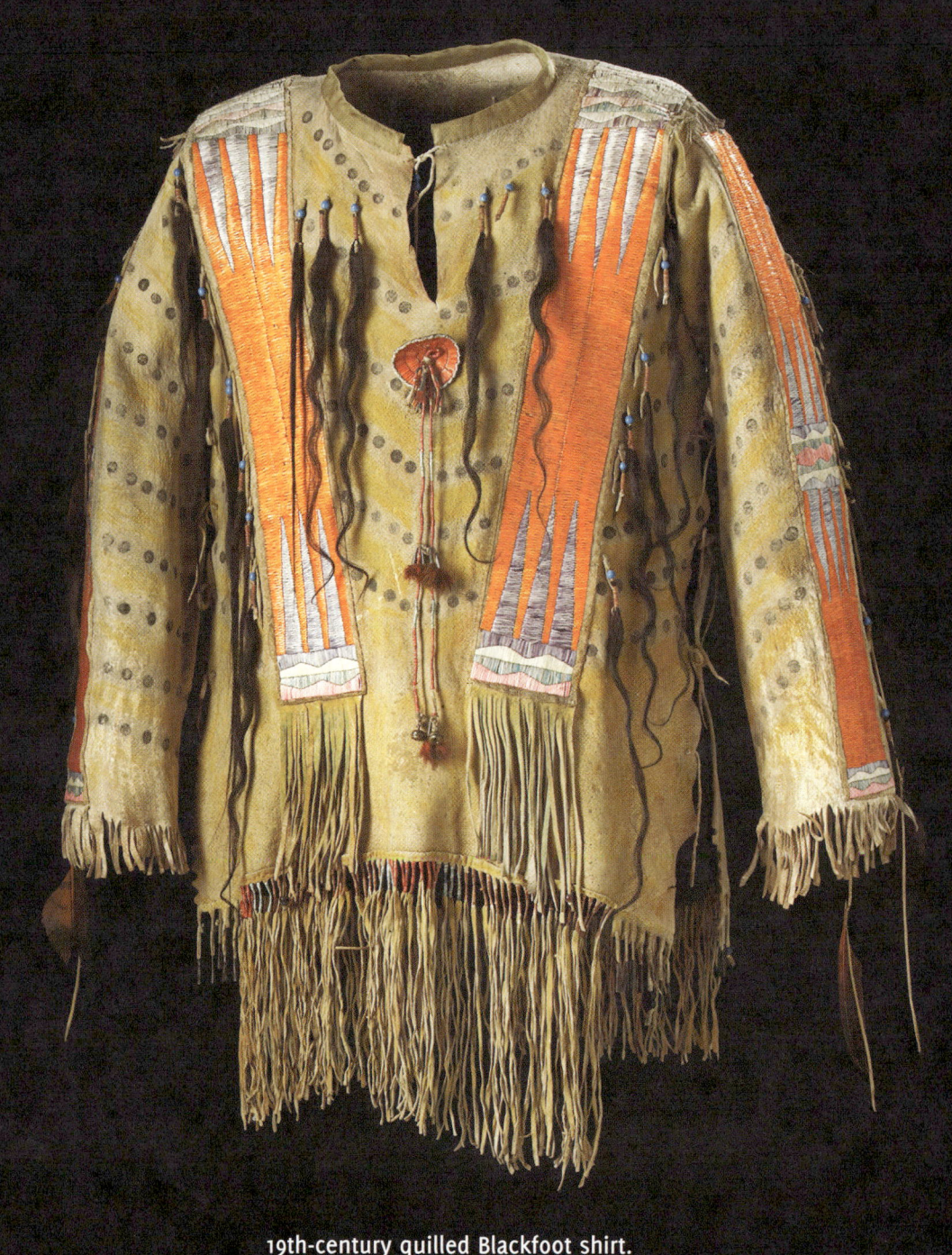

19th-century quilled Blackfoot shirt.
*Dyed porcupine quills were woven into designs
that had a special meaning for the owner.*

AUGUST

22 **1838.** Charles Grant, 1st Baron Glenelg—Lord Glenelg, Secretary in the Parliament of Britain, ordered an investigation and report on the living conditions of Mi'kmaq in Nova Scotia, which revealed a declining population and miserable circumstances.

23 **1978.** Métis leader Harry Daniels testified before the Special Joint Committee of the Senate and House of Commons on the Constitution. He identified the Manitoba Act as the document that confirmed the Métis as one of the founding peoples of Confederation.

24 **1977.** The Federation of Saskatchewan Indian Nations and the Governments of Canada and Saskatchewan achieved a preliminary agreement for land promised in treaties.

25 **2001.** Fishing Lake First Nation representatives signed the Fishing Lake 1907 Surrender Settlement Agreement compensating the band for 13,170 acres of land surrendered to the Government of Canada in 1907.

26 **1971.** At Eskasoni First Nation, Basil Joe, 13-year-old son of Mi'kmaw poet Rita Joe, rescued 4-year-old Bridget Marshall, who was drowning. Joe received the Royal Canadian Humane Association's Bronze Medal for Bravery for his leadership in the rescue.

27 **1949.** Beatrice Mosioner (née Culletin), Métis author, was born in St. Boniface, Manitoba.

28 **1988.** The majority of the members of the Association of Métis and Non-status Indians of Saskatchewan (AMNSIS) voted affirmatively to restore the organization to a Métis political body. Thus AMNSIS became once again the Métis Society of Saskatchewan.

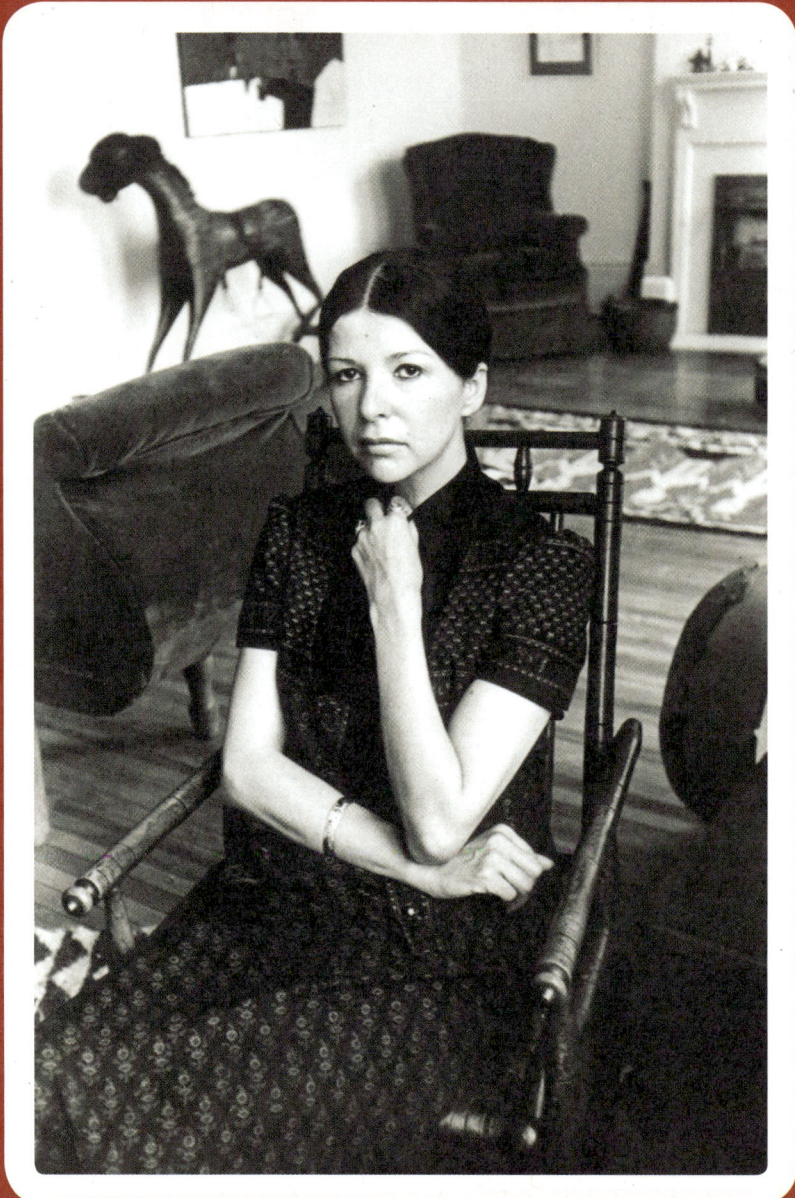

Alanis Obomsawin, 1971.
See August 31.

AUGUST

29

30   **2004**. Métis artist Bob Boyer died.

31   **1932**. Alanis Obomsawin, Abenaki filmmaker and singer, born.

"From a grain of sand to a great mountain, all is sacred."

—PETER BLUE CLOUD, MOHAWK WRITER

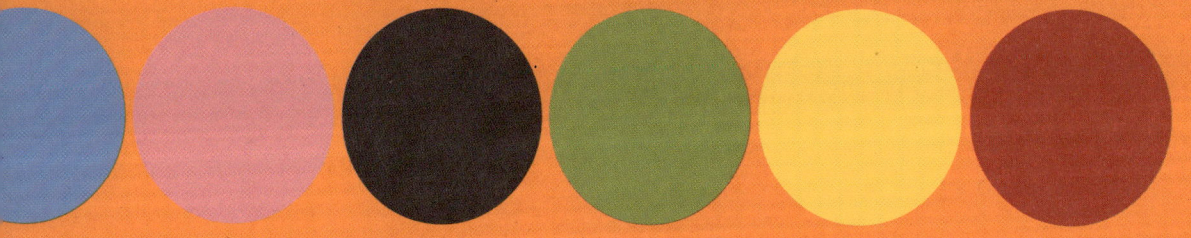

- **1545:** Jacques Cartier published the first known vocabulary of First Nations words (of Laurentian, a now-extinct branch of the Iroquoian language family). One of the words included in the list is "canada," the Laurentian word for "village."

- **1888** (September 18): Archibald Stansfeld Belaney (better known as "Grey Owl") was born in Hastings, England.

- **1939** (September 10): Canada entered the Second World War. Over 3,000 First Nations men and women would serve in the Canadian Army during the course of the war.

- **1993** (September 15): The Mi'kmaw Grand Council met for the time in almost 100 years—its last meeting had been held at Big Cove, New Brunswick, in 1902.

september
manoominike-giizis
(ANISHINAABE)
"Rice Moon"

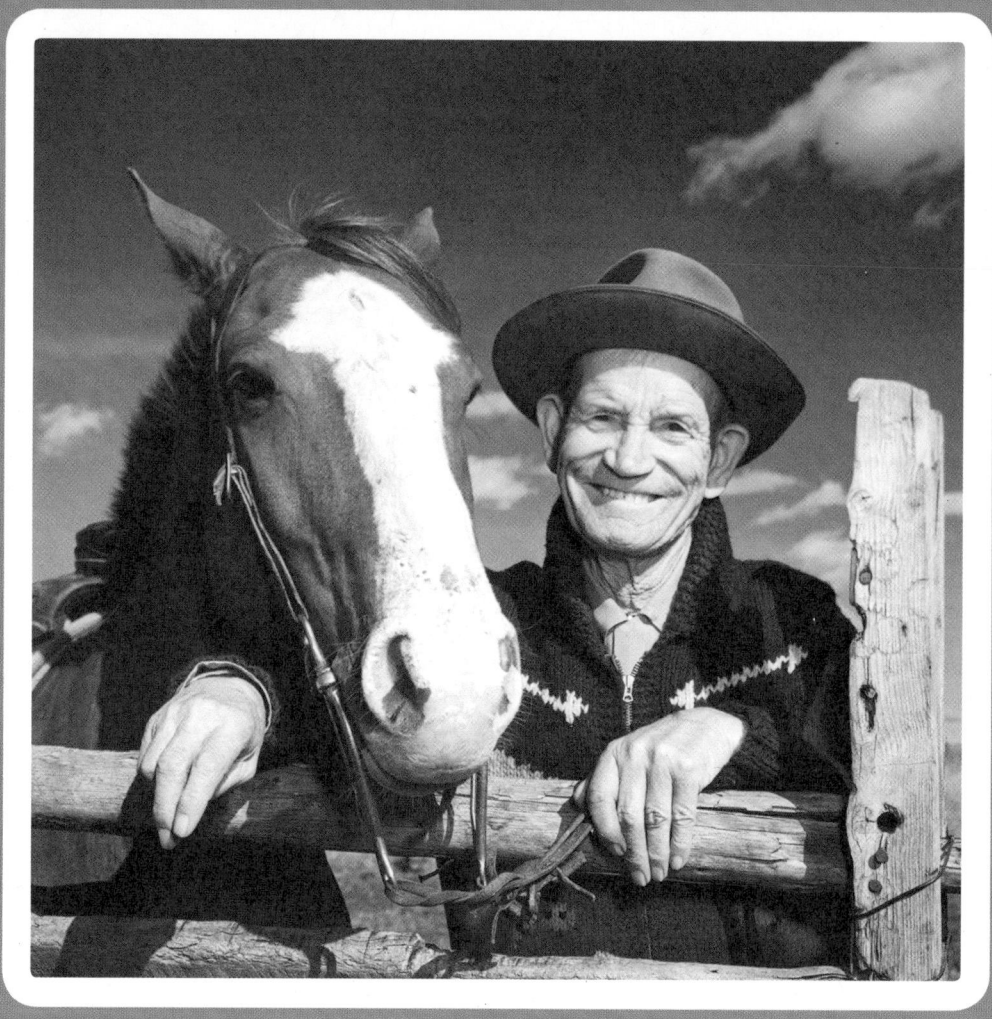

James Gladstone (1887–1971).
See September 4.

SEPTEMBER

1 **1999.** The Aboriginal Peoples Television Network began broadcasting across Canada; it replaced Television Northern Canada.

2 **1981.** The United Nations ruled that Canada's Indian Act violated international human rights by discriminating on the basis of gender.

3

4 **1971.** Akay-na-muka (Many Guns), James Gladstone died at Fernie, British Columbia. In 1958, on the advice of Prime Minister John Diefenbaker, Gladstone was the first Status Indian to be appointed to the Canadian Senate, two years before full federal voting rights were granted to Canada's Native peoples. He served in the Senate for 13 years.

5 **2008.** The Honourable Chuck Strahl, Minister of Indian Affairs and Northern Development and Federal Interlocutor for Métis and Non-status Indians, announced the signing of a protocol with the Métis National Council.

6 **2004.** Métis activist Harry Daniels died.

7 **1937.** Albert Bellegarde, future chief of the Federation of Saskatchewan Indian Nations, was born.

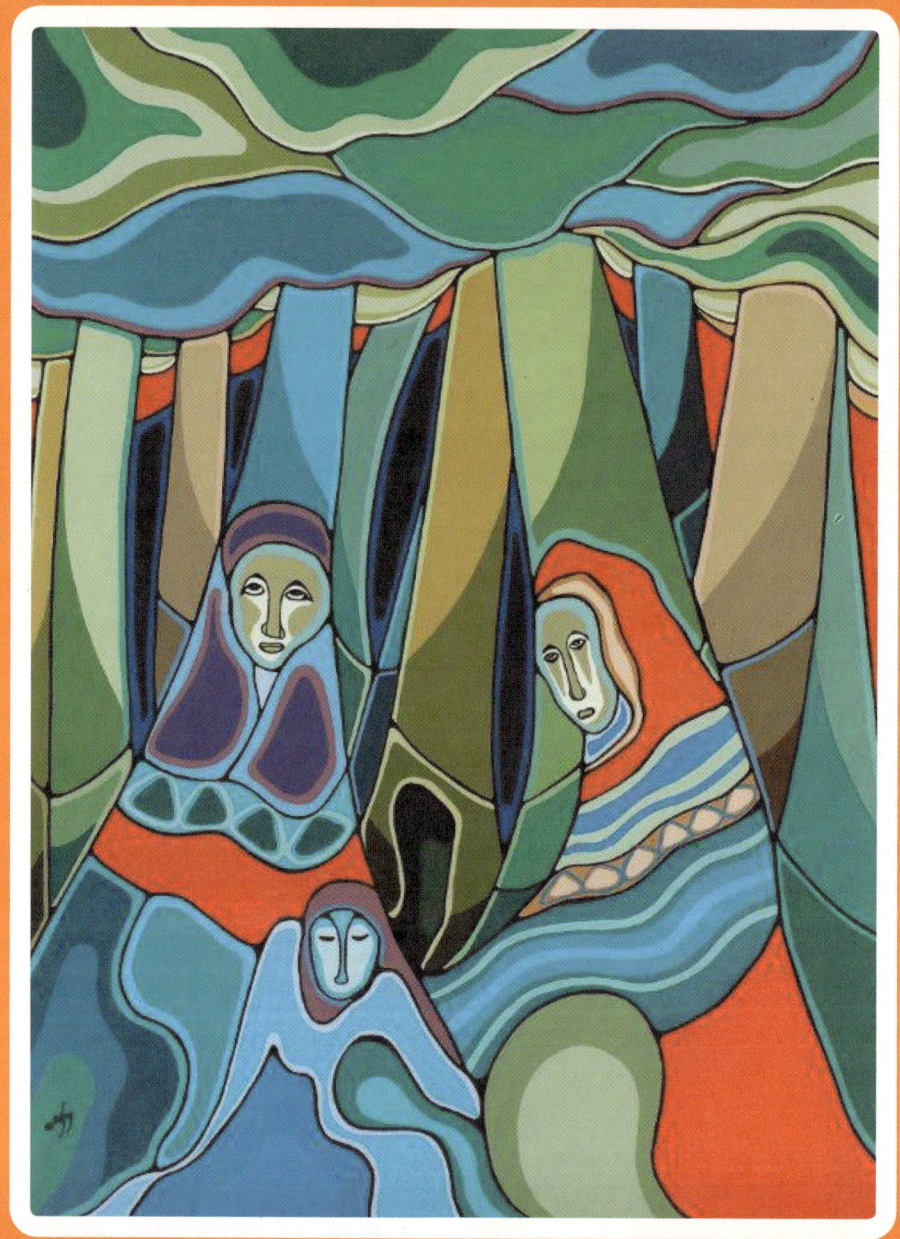

Daphne Odjig, *The Oneness of it All.*
Acrylic on canvas, 137 x 102 centimetres, 1985.
See September 11.

SEPTEMBER

8 1874. Negotiations for Treaty 4 (the Qu'Appelle Treaty) began. In 1915 the monument pictured here was unveiled in Fort Qu'Appelle at the site of the original treaty signing. ▶

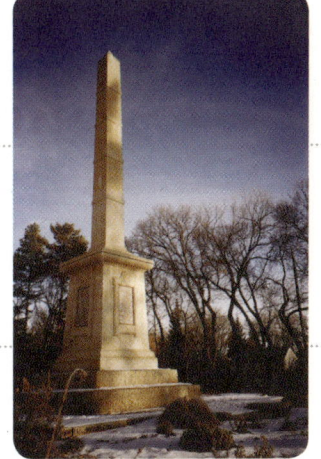

9 1875. Okanis, first Chief of the Okanese First Nation in Saskatchewan, signed adhesion to Treaty 4.

10 1874. Representatives of the Queen promised First Nations negotiators of Treaty 4 schoolmasters on reserve.

11 1919. Daphne Odjig, Ottawa-Potawatomi artist, recipient of two honourary degrees and a Member of the Order of Canada, was born at Wikwemikong, Ontario.

12 1875. Adhesion to Treaty 3 enabled the Métis of Fort Francis, Ontario, to take treaty.

13 2007. The United Nations General Assembly adopted the United Nations Declaration on the Rights of Indigenous Peoples. Canada voted against its adoption.

14 1914. Reporter and politician Mervin Dieter was born at the File Hills Colony on the Peepeekisis Reserve in Saskathewan.

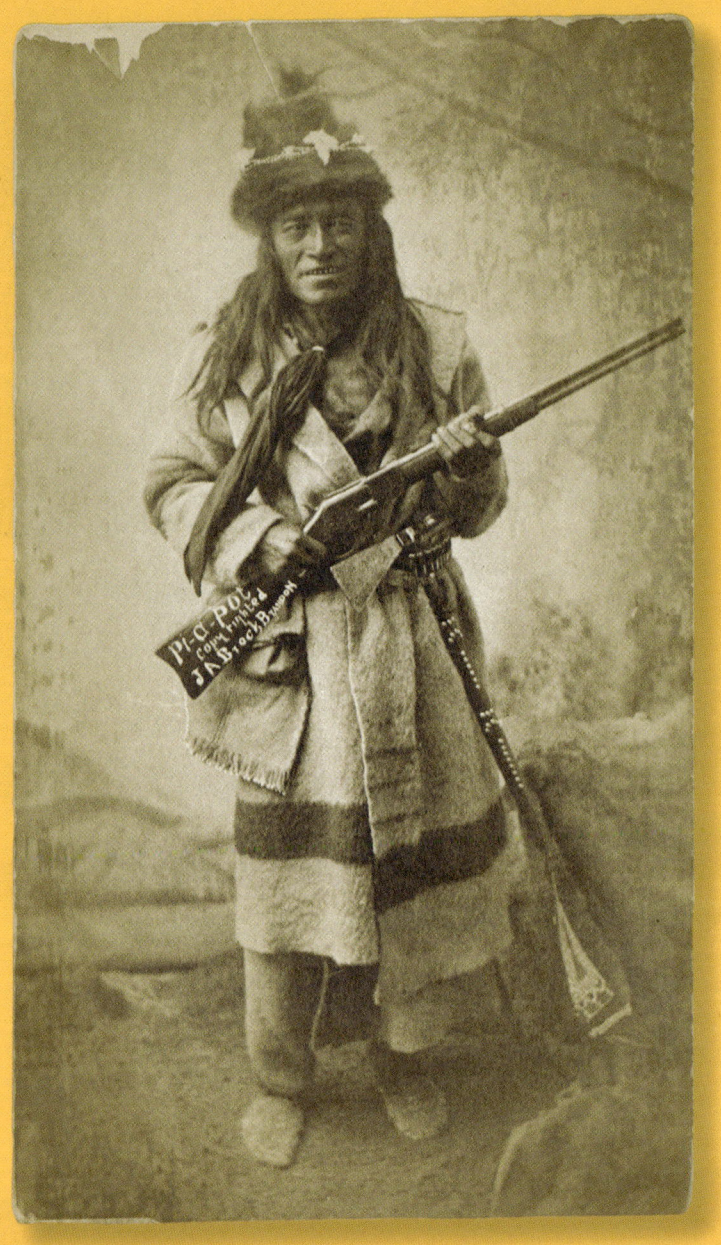

Chief Piapot (1816-1908).
See September 17.

SEPTEMBER

15 **1874.** First Nations Chiefs signed Treaty 4 at Fort Qu'Appelle, Saskatchewan, between Her Majesty the Queen of Great Britain and the Cree and Saulteaux of the Qu'Appelle Valley.

16 **1940.** Harry Daniels, Métis political leader, was born at Regina Beach, Saskatchewan.

17 **1883.** Legend has it that Chief Piapot (Payepot), Cree leader, temporarily delayed the construction of the Canadian Pacific Railway near the present-day community of Piapot, Saskatchewan.

18 **1611.** Mi'kmaw Grand Chief Membertou died in what is now known as Digby County, Nova Scotia. His exact age is unknown, but he was a grown man when he met Jacques Cartier in 1534.

19 **2003.** The Supreme Court of Canada ruled in *R v. Powley* in favour of a Métis Aboriginal right to harvest.

20 **2007.** The Truth and Reconciliation Commission officially began its mandate.

21 **1985.** The Inuit Circumpolar Conference concluded in Montreal. The Conference called for the Government of Canada to pay more attention to Inuit unity, dignity, political rights, and economic self-sufficiency.

Assembly of First Nations

From the time when Canada became a nation to the present, First Nations have sought not only to be recognized by the federal government but also to ensure their representation within the government structure. This process has not been easy. In 1927, a revised Indian Act made it illegal for First Nations to organize politically. From 1927 until the repeal of these punitive provisions in 1951, if First Nations leaders sought political organization they were jailed. This prosecution, coupled with enforced attendance in Residential Schools and the banning of potlatches, meant that First Nations experienced difficulties attempting to act in their own political interest. The first attempt at creating a political presence was the formation of the League of Indians in Canada, during World War I. However, due to strong oppression from the government, the League was not able to grow and attract national attention and soon disbanded. Another attempt at forming a lobby organization occurred in the 1940s when the North American Indian Brotherhood (NAIB) was formed. But like the League of Indians before it, the NAIB failed to garner support and fell apart. In 1961, the National Indian Council (NIC) was created to represent the Status or Treaty people, those who were non-Status, and the Métis (the Inuit were excluded). However, creating a unified message for three often politically disparate groups proved difficult and, by 1968, the NIC split by mutual agreement. The non-Status and Métis formed the Native Council of Canada; the Status and Treaty people became the National Indian Brotherhood (NIB). The NIB became the strongest group yet, and by the early 1970s was a political presence on national and international levels, bringing issues such as housing, health care, and First Nations self-governance to the forefront. However, the NIB still had difficulty acting on behalf of Canada's entire First Nations population. Accused of not adequately representing their people, the NIB restructured in 1982 and became the Assembly of First Nations (AFN). The AFN has worked most notably to bring the issue of self-governance forward and has participated in four constitutional conferences to address this issue. They have also worked to change policies regarding land claims, education and treaty rights. (JAMES OSTIME)

SEPTEMBER

22 **1992.** The Saulteaux First Nation in Saskatchewan signed the Treaty Land Entitlement Framework Agreement.

23 **1982.** The Federation of Métis Settlements President Elmer Ghostkeeper argued, in a letter to the Native Council of Canada and its provincial affiliates, that the time had come for the Métis to separate from the organization in order to define their distinct identity for upcoming constitutional conferences.

24 **1993.** Walter Twin, Sawridge Chief, launched a court challenge to Bill C-31.

25 **1998.** *My Flesh the Sound of Rain*, by Métis poet Heather MacLeod, was published by Coteau Books, Regina, Saskatchewan. ▶

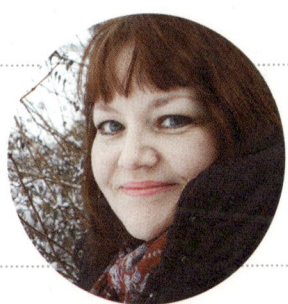

26 **2002.** The Métis National Council adopted a national definition of citizenship.

27

28 **1663.** The sale of liquor to Aboriginals was prohibited in Quebec City.

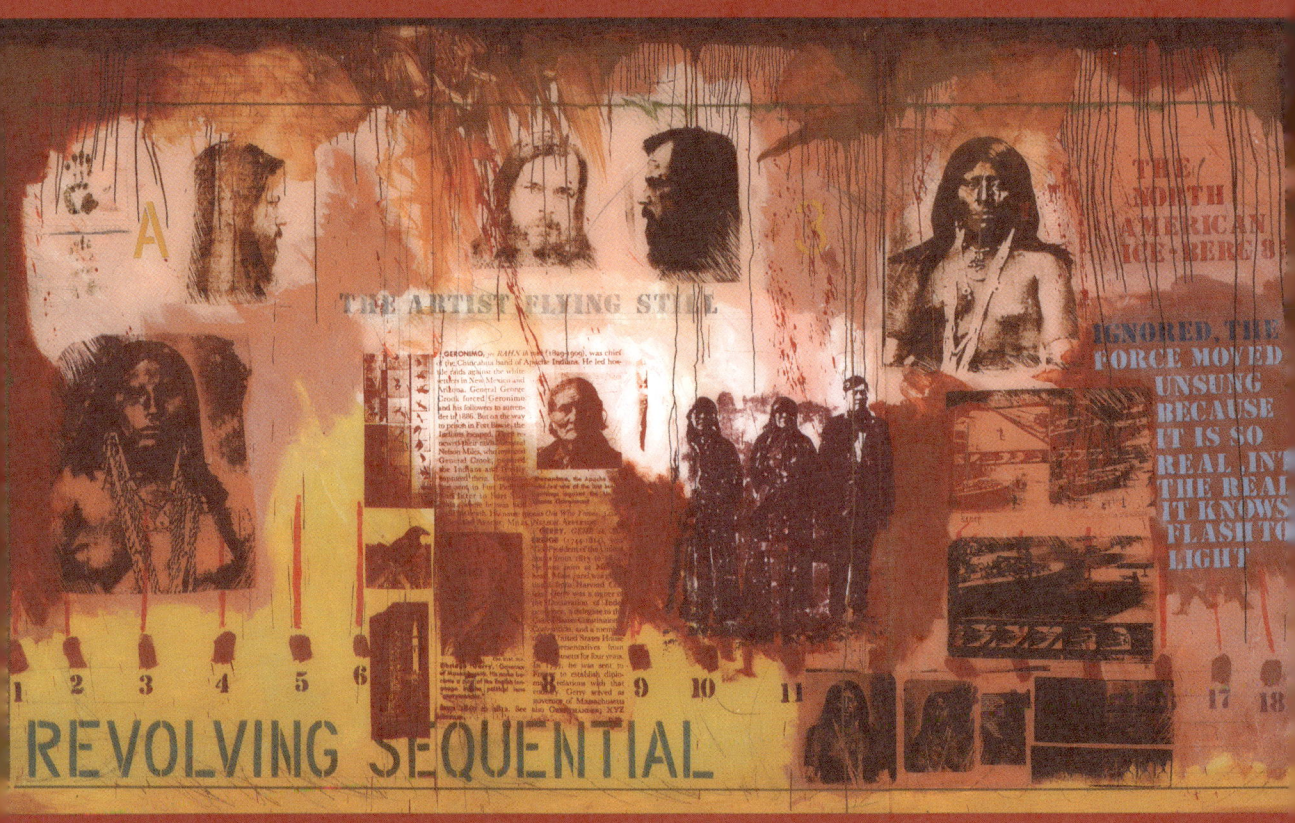

Carl Beam, *The North American Iceberg.*
Acrylic, photo-serigraph, and graphite on Plexiglas, 213.6 x 374.1 centimetres, 1985.

SEPTEMBER

29 **1983.** The Glenwood Mi'kmaq First Nation in Newfoundland opened the first Mi'kmaw commercial smoke tannery in Gander.

30 **1949.** Marie Battiste, Mi'kmaw educator, administrator, curriculum developer, and activist was born.

"The white man who is our agent is so stingy that he carries a linen rag in his pocket into which to blow his nose, for fear he might blow away something of value."

—PAYEPOT, CREE CHIEF

- **1991:** Prime Minister Brian Mulroney recognized the Métis as a nation within the Canadian Federation.

- **2005:** Over 800 members of the Kashechewan First Nation near James Bay, Ontario, were evacuated after the E. coli bacteria was discovered in their water supply system.

- **2007:** The Métis of southeast Saskatchewan won the right to hunt, fish, and trap in the Qu'Appelle Valley.

- **2010:** The five First Nations of the Maa-nulth First Nations voted in favour of accepting the Maa-nulth Final Agreement—the first modern-day treaty for Vancouver Island and the second under the British Columbia Treaty Commission process.

october

kentenha
(MOHAWK)

"Little Poor Time"

The Story of Tecumseh

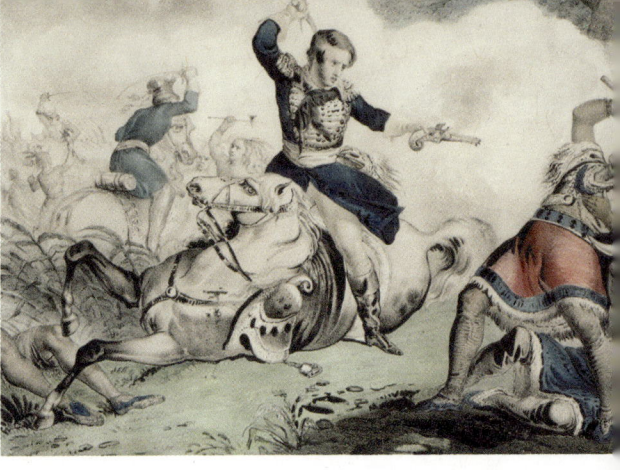

Nathanial Currier, Death of Tecumseh. *Lithograph, coloured by hand, 1846.*

Tecumseh was born in 1768 in what is now Ohio. Of the Shawnee tribe, he experienced the displacement common to Native Americans of the time. In 1768, the Iroquois, who claimed the land where the Shawnee resided, sold it to the British, and from approximately 1774 to 1782 armies invaded the land the Shawnee considered theirs. The Shawnee were too small a nation to defend their land, and their population fell to approximately 1,000 when Tecumseh's father, a chief, was killed in 1774. In 1785 the Shawnee signed a treaty surrendering this land to the U.S. government, and several battles followed where Tecumseh proved himself a great warrior. As battles raged on and further treaties were signed (many of which were unfair and achieved through intimidation of Native Americans), Tecumseh took the stance he is remembered for today. Land, he argued, was no more a property of the people than air or water, and on that basis, Tecumseh refused to sign subsequent treaties. As his reputation as an orator grew, so did his message of unification of Native Americans. After seeing small tribes like the Shawnee bow to the pressure of the U.S. government, he urged tribes to stop fighting each other and unite against their white oppressors. He began organizing a confederation to resist pressure from U.S. citizens and travelled throughout the country with his message of unity. Tecumseh was a formidable presence in the War of 1812, in what was then known as Upper Canada, having allied with both First Nations and British forces against the U.S. He fought in the Battle of Lake Erie in 1813 and fought in the Battle of the Thames later that year, but it was during this later battle that Tecumseh was killed, shot as he charged forward with his comrades. Tecumseh did not consider himself a Canadian hero nor a British or U.S. one; his concern was the unification of First Nations, regardless of what country they were in, against oppressive forces that threatened their livelihoods, a cause for which he fought to the death. (JAMES OSTIME)

OCTOBER

1   **2004.** The Government of Alberta, the Métis Nation of Alberta, and the Métis Settlements General Council signed the Interim Métis Harvesting Agreement, which recognized the harvesting rights of the Métis in the province. The effect of the Agreement was that Alberta had been recognized by its government as an historical Métis homeland.

2   **2002.** Daniel N. Paul, Mi'kmaw author and journalist, was inducted into the Order of Nova Scotia.

3   **1927.** Kenojuak Ashevak, Inuit artist and sculptor, was born at Ikerasak, Baffin Island, Northwest Territories (now Nunavut).

4

5   **1813.** Tecumseh (Shooting Star), Shawnee war chief, was killed in battle.

6   **1862.** The Manitoulin Island Treaty was signed.

7   **1763.** King George III of Britain issued a Royal Proclamation establishing the territory acquired by the British after the Seven Years War and set a foundation for Native-newcomer relations under British rule.

The Potlatch

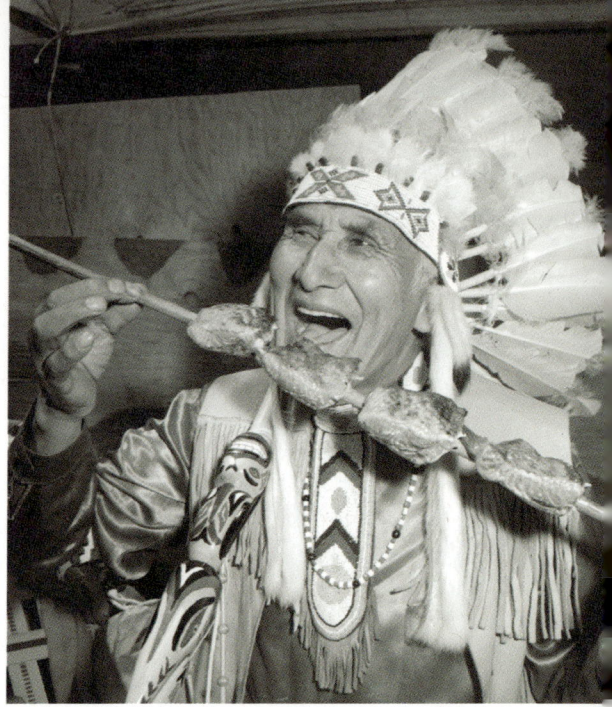

Chief Dan George eating salmon from a skewer at a potlatch in 1966.

The potlatch is a ceremony once practised frequently among First Nations along the northwest coast of Canada. It helped to establish rank and status as well as bestow land and goods to the people from various bands and nations who would assemble at the site of the ceremony. Typically, a potlatch ceremony was preceded by extensive preparation that often involved ritual fasting and theatrical performances, dances and songs, and, most significantly, the distribution of goods, foodstuffs, land, and even slaves among the participants. To host a potlatch was to assert one's power and status as much as to bestow it upon others. In these ceremonies, wealth was determined not by who received the most goods but by who gave the most away. As such, the goods were often ritualistically destroyed after they were distributed, to emphasize the significance of the gesture of giving, not the materials. This ritual destruction inherent to the potlatch became problematic to the Canadian government because one band would trade land to another and then that property was often destroyed. Ironically, it was the European explorers who first arrived in what is now North America who introduced the concept of land as a commodity to First Nations who lived there. To curb what they saw as a barbaric and needlessly destructive practice, the Canadian government made potlatch ceremonies illegal in 1884. Despite the new law, some bands continued to practice the ceremony covertly and smaller in scope so as to avoid detection until the law was repealed by the Canadian government in 1951. Since then, efforts have been made to revitalize the tradition but, because the practice was suppressed for so long, the potlatch is no longer the grand ceremony it once was. (JAMES OSTIME)

OCTOBER

8

9 **1986.** Nova Scotia Attorney General Ron Giffin announced the convening of a public inquiry into the wrongful conviction of Donald Marshall, Jr.

10 **1992.** The first Canadian Native Haute Cuisine gold medal team arrived at the 92-year-old World Culinary Olympics at Frankfurt, Germany; the team won 7 gold, 2 silver, and 3 bronze medals.

11 **1869.** A party of Métis with Louis Riel stopped the survey of the Red River Settlement.

12 **1972.** The first exhibit of Mi'kmaw, Maliseet, Iroquois, Woodland Cree, Plains Cree, Sioux, Blackfoot, Nootka, and Inuit artifacts opened at the Museum of Nova Scotia.

13 **1972.** A plaque honouring Poundmaker was unveiled at the Cut Knife battlefield site on the Poundmaker Reserve in Saskatchewan.

14 **1923.** Métis activist and leader Charles Trotchie was born at Round Prairie, Saskatchewan.

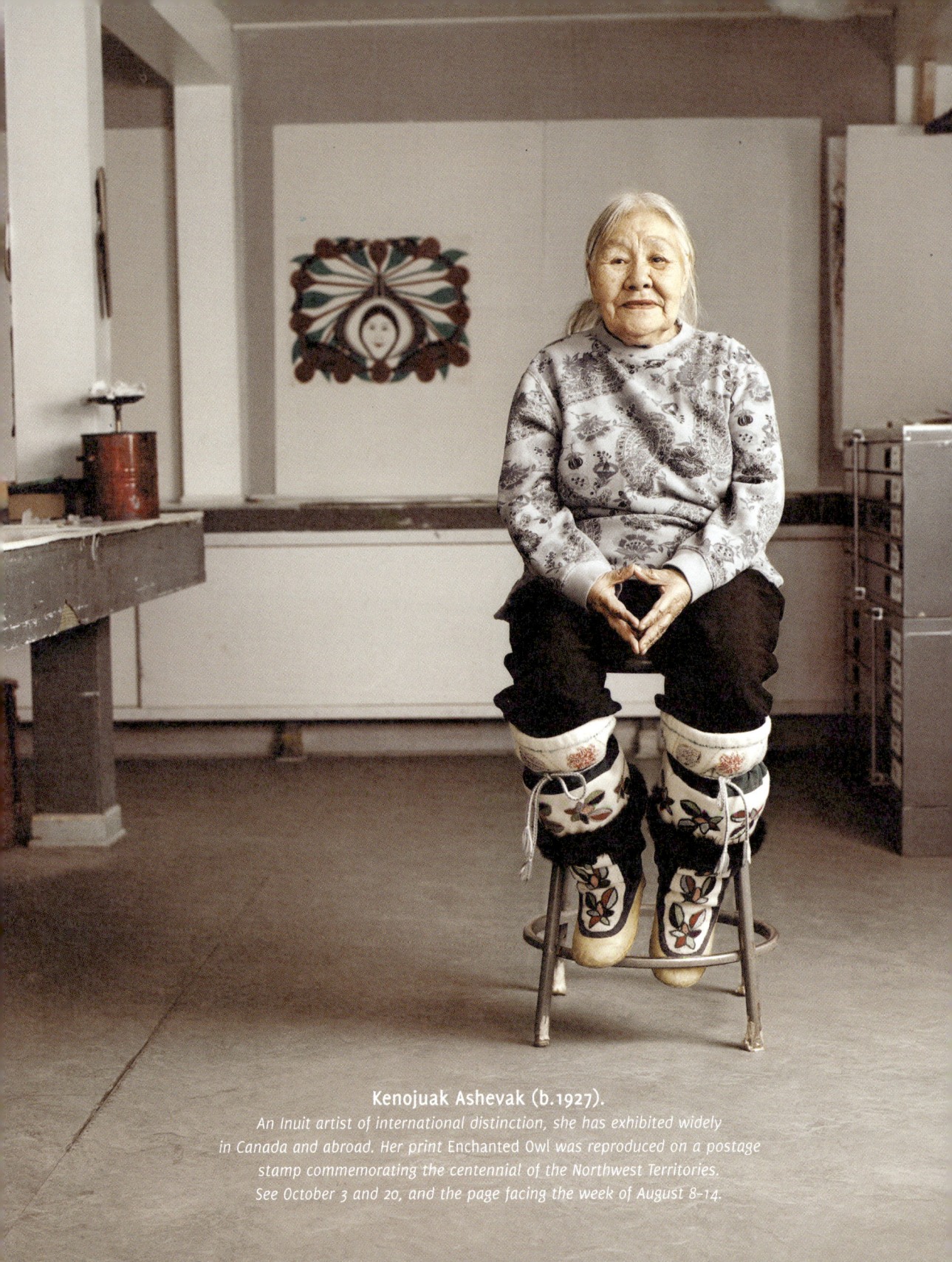

Kenojuak Ashevak (b. 1927).
An Inuit artist of international distinction, she has exhibited widely in Canada and abroad. Her print Enchanted Owl was reproduced on a postage stamp commemorating the centennial of the Northwest Territories. See October 3 and 20, and the page facing the week of August 8–14.

OCTOBER

15 **1889.** Richard Hardisty, chief factor of the Hudson's Bay Company, and member of the Canadian Senate (1888-89) died in Winnipeg, Manitoba, from injuries suffered in a horse and buggy accident. ▶

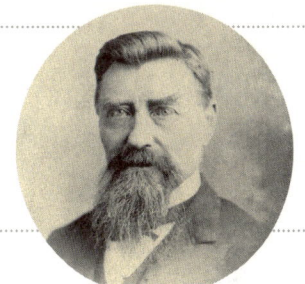

16 **1988.** At the Métis National Council annual assembly in Edmonton, Alberta, Yvon Dumont was elected President of the Council. He would be the first national President of the body made up of representatives from the provincial Métis associations in Canada.

17 **1986.** Nine Aboriginal constables graduated from the Atlantic Police Academy at Holland College in Charlottetown, Prince Edward Island.

18 **1965.** Abraham Okpik was the first Inuit appointed to the Northwest Territories Council.

19 **1983.** The Federation of Saskatchewan Indian Nations held its first Legislative Assembly of Chiefs.

20 **2008.** Justice Harry LaForme resigned as Chair of the Truth and Reconciliation Commission.

1982. Cape Dorset artist Kenojuak Ashevak was invested as a Companion of the Order of Canada.

21 **1998.** *Lady of Silences*, by Cree playwright Floyd Favel Starr, opened at the Globe Theatre, Regina, Saskatchewan.

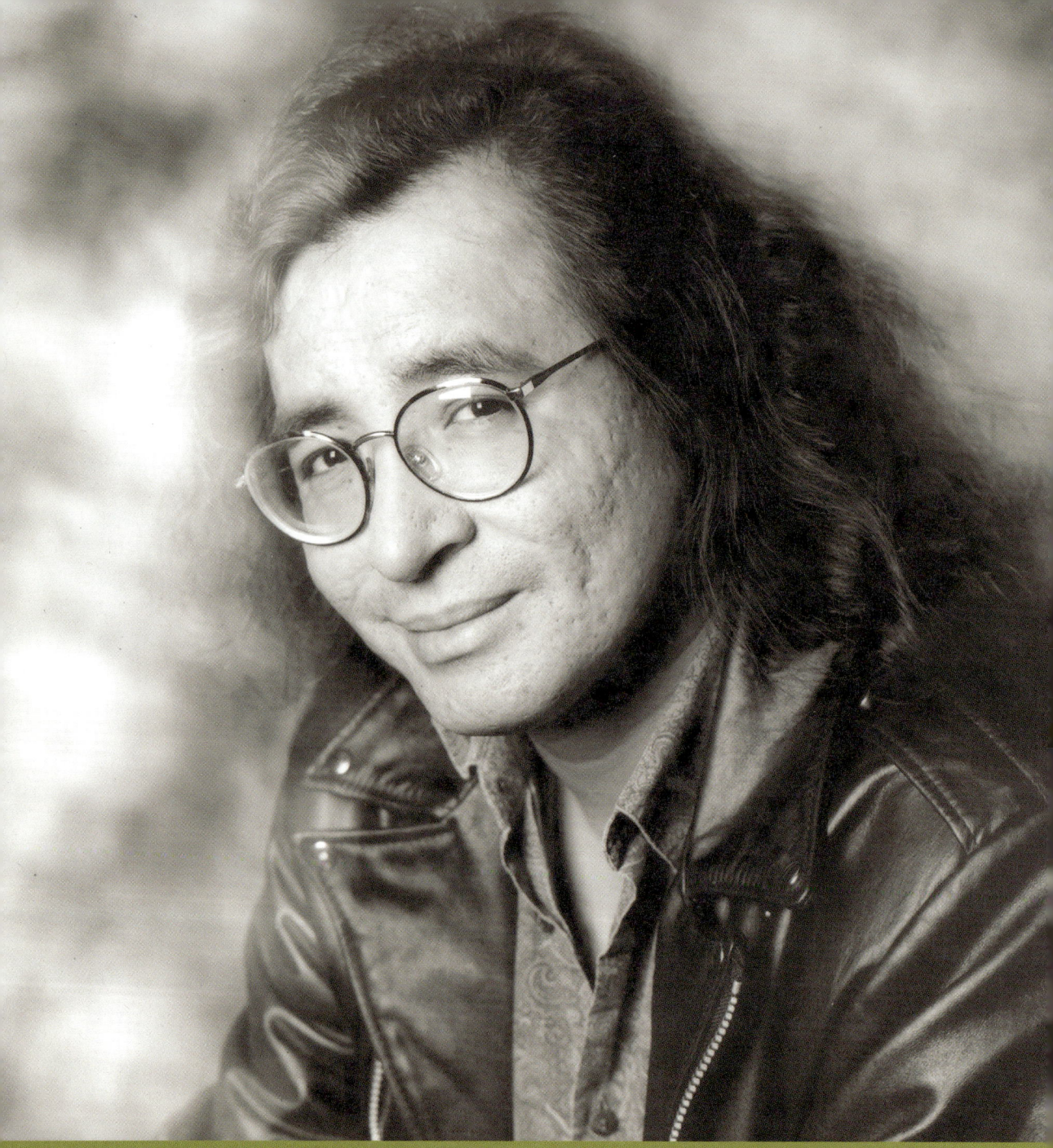

Tomson Highway (b. 1951).
Tomson Highway's formidable talents as a playwright, producer, and director reflect the richness of Native people's culture and spirituality. See October 27 and December 6.

OCTOBER

22 — **1993.** Métis hunters Steve and Roddy Powley were arrested after killing a bull moose near Sault Ste. Marie, Ontario.

23

24 — **2003.** Métis National Council delegates elected Clément Chartier as president of the Métis National Council.

25 — **1985.** Aboriginals in Grande Cache, Alberta, protested an order against hunting arguing that hunting is a right, not a privilege.

26

27 — **1948.** Tom Jackson, Cree actor and singer, was born. Jackson is currently the Chancellor of Trent University.   **1993.** Tomson Highway was awarded Membership in the Order of Canada.

28 — **1678.** The ban on the sale of liquor to Aboriginals was lifted in New France.

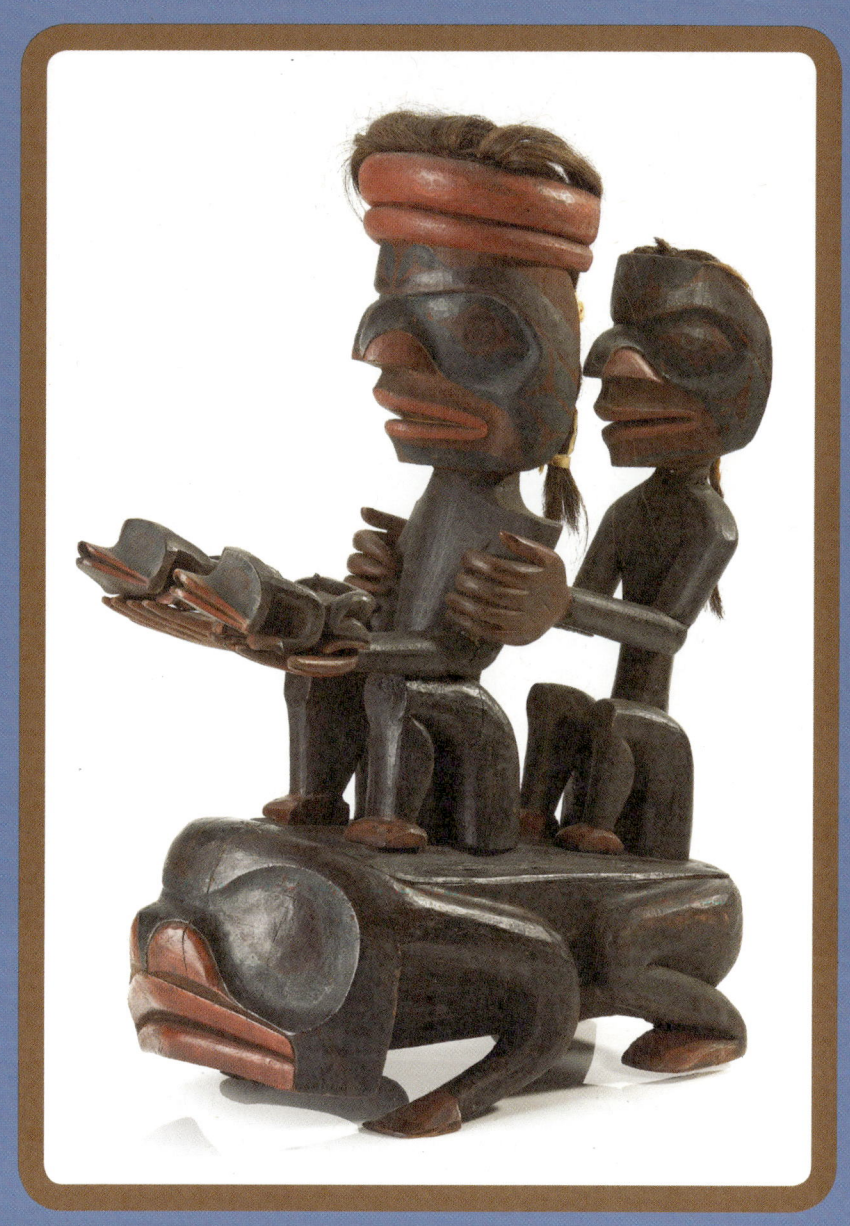

Two Figures on a Frog.
This finely-carved Heiltsuk figure was collected on the west coast in the 1860s by British naval captain Sir William Wiseman; it remained in his family for many years.

OCTOBER

29

30 **1917.** Famed long-distance runner Alex Decoteau was killed at Passchendaele, Belgium.

2008. Leona Aglukkaq, from Nunavut, was sworn in as Canada's Health Minister.

31

"*Never* sit
while your elders stand."
—CREE SAYING

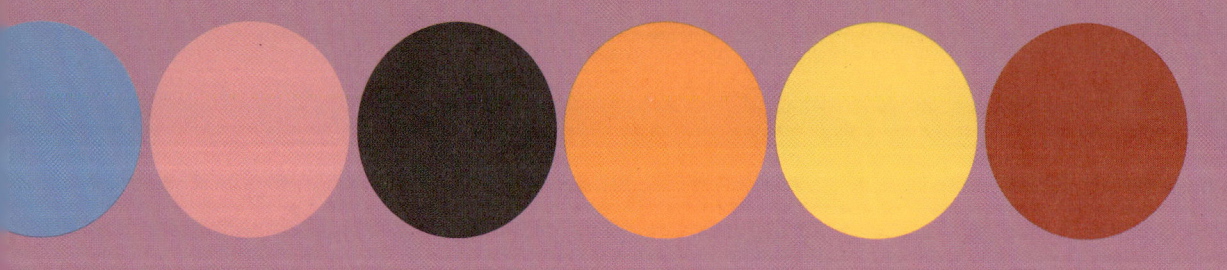

- **c. 1510:** Mi'kmaw Grand Chief Membertou was born. Membertou lived to be approximately 100 years of age, and is the only individual known to have met both Jacques Cartier (1534) and Samuel de Champlain (1605).

- **1607–1615:** The "Tarrateen War" took place between the Mi'kmaq and Abenaki over the fur trade with the French. The Mi'kmaq were victorious in the war; warriors killed Abenaki leader Onemechin in contemporary Maine.

- **1876:** The Sioux, eventually including Sitting Bull, began entering Canada to escape American retribution following the Battle of Little Big Horn. Sitting Bull and most of the Sioux returned to the United States in 1881.

- **1905–06:** Treaty 9 (the "James Bay Treaty") was signed between the federal government and various Cree and Ojibwe peoples of northern Ontario and Quebec.

november
keptekewiku's
(MI'KMAW)
"Frost Month"

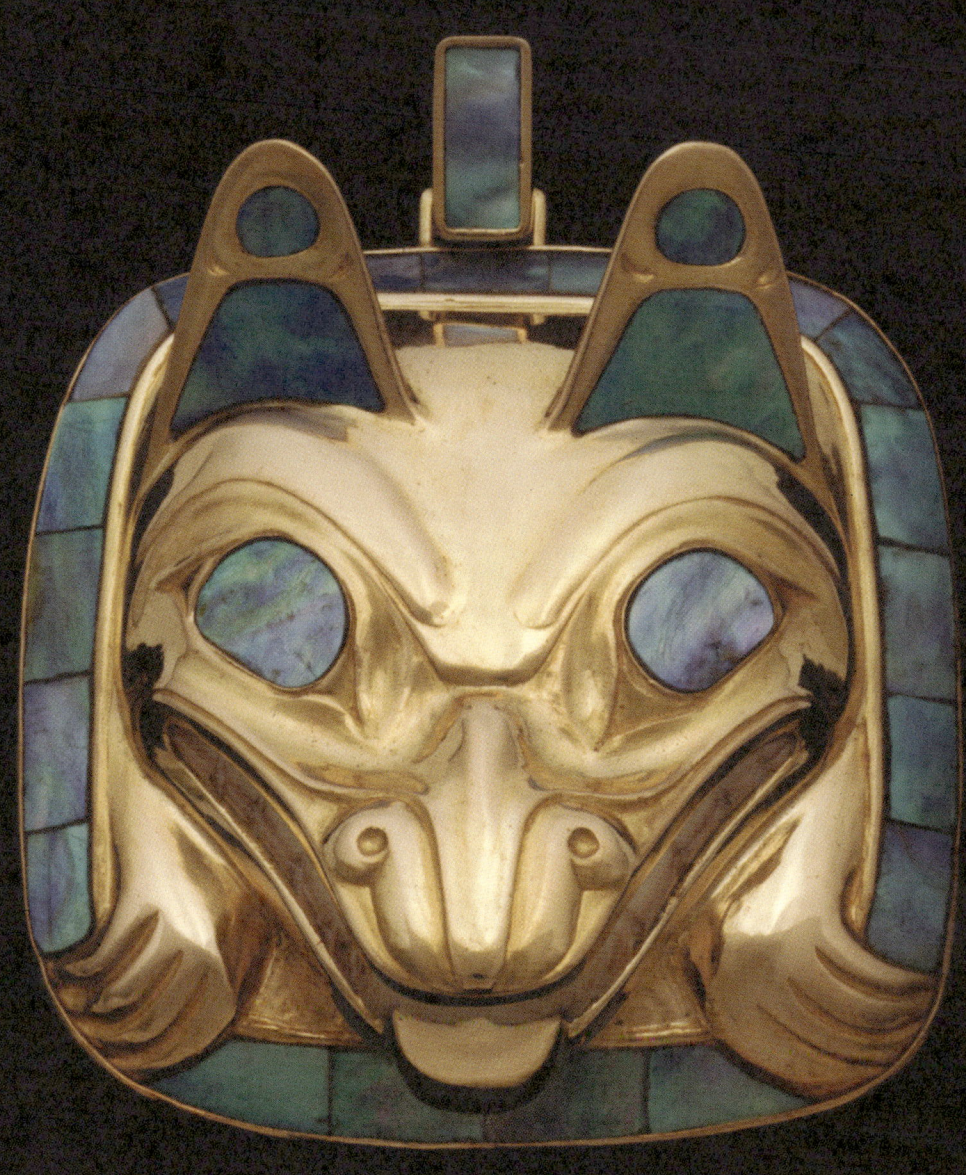

Bill Reid (1920-98), *Wolf pendant*.
*22K gold and abalone shell (haliotis) inlay, 4 x 4 x 1.5 centimetres, 1976.
See January 12, July 5, November 5, and the page facing the week of November 15-20.*

NOVEMBER

1   **1994.** Carol Sanderson, Cree educator, was awarded the Saskatchewan Order of Merit for her work in First Nations education.

2   **1990.** The first edition of the *Micmac-Maliseet Nations News* published.

3   **2006.** The Gary Tinker Federation for the Disabled, based in La Ronge, Saskatchewan, received a provincial Spirit Award for Community-Based Organizations.

4   **1946.** Guud San Glans (Eagle of the Dawn), Robert Charles Davidson, Haida artist and great-grandson of Charles Edenshaw, was born in Hydaburg, Alaska.

5   **1974.** A Bill Reid retrospective with 200 of the Haida artist's works, opened at the Vancouver Art Gallery in Vancouver, British Columbia.

6

7

First Nations Participation in World Wars I and II

In the early 20th century, the relationship between the Canadian government and First Nations was decidedly strained. There were treaties, policies, and laws imposed by government that limited the rights and freedoms of First Nations. However, as the country faced two world wars, every major battle was fought with the help of First Nations, and their contributions were immeasurable. Regardless of their actual citizenship in Canada, First Nations were considered British subjects by the Crown in times of war. However, some First Nations believed themselves marginalized in light of the Indian Act, and decided against enlistment. Others saw war as an equalizer, believing that fighting alongside other Canadians would earn them the rights and freedoms they sought. Despite these conflicting views, First Nations participated in both wars in high numbers. In World War II, there were at least 3,000 treaty or Status Indians enlisted, including 72 women. There were also a large number of Inuit, Métis, and non-status Indians involved. Returning home, many First

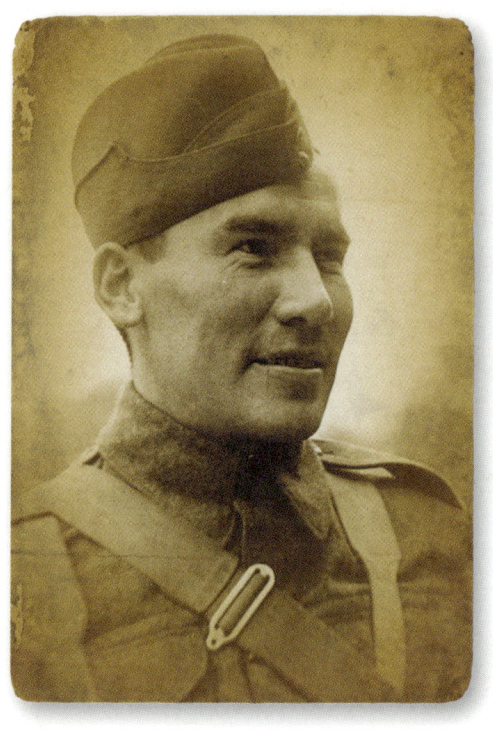

Sergeant Harvey Dreaver, son of Chief Joe Dreaver of the Mistawasis Band in Saskatchewan, was killed in action in 1944 during the battle at the Leopold Canal. He was buried at Adegem Canadian War Cemetery in Belgium.

Nations veterans had a different perspective on their role as citizens of Canada. They had fought, bled, and died alongside other Canadians and began to believe strongly in their own rights in the country. Many became community leaders and began to organize politically on behalf of their own rights. They were proud Canadians, had defended the country in both world wars, and believed their status within Canada was worth fighting for. (JAMES OSTIME)

NOVEMBER

8

1752. Mi'kmaw chief Major Jean-Baptiste Cope of Subenacadie concluded a treaty with the Nova Scotia governor stating that all warlike events between the British and Mi'kmaq should be buried in oblivion with the hatchet.

9

1849. Métis and Ojibwe from Sault Ste. Marie captured a mining camp at Mica Bay on Lake Superior.

2009. Three young people—Anthony Arreak, Lucassie Tukkiapik, and Cindy Koneak—carried the Olympic torch through Kuujjuaq, Nunavik, Quebec.

10

11

1972. Mary McLeod became the first Aboriginal woman to be named Canada's Memorial Cross Mother, placing a wreath at the National War Memorial in Ottawa on Remembrance Day on behalf of all Canadian mothers who had lost children to the war. Two of her sons died in World War II.

12

1925. Agnes Nanogak, Inuit graphic artist and storyteller, was born on Baillie Island, Northwest Territories.

13

14

Bill Reid

Bill Reid (1920-1998) is widely considered to be one of Canada's greatest artists. His proud artistic depictions reflecting his Haida heritage are known throughout North America and the world but might never have existed had his mother continued to keep her heritage a secret, as she had done when Bill was a child. Reid was born and spent his childhood in Victoria, British Columbia. He was born to a European father and a Haida mother. Reid was raised in the western culture of his contemporaries, and his mother did not divulge her Haida roots until he was a teenager, perhaps to spare him the social stigma of that time associated with "half-breeds" (children born of one European or white parent and one First Nations parent). As an adult, Reid embraced his Haida ancestry and, in his twenties, travelled to the Queen Charlotte Islands where his mother was born and where his grandfather still lived. He watched his grandfather carve and was undoubtedly influenced, as he began carving himself. The sculptures he would eventually create include *Raven and the First Men*, *The Spirit of Haida Gwaii* and, perhaps his most famous piece, *Lootaas*, a fifteen-metre canoe carved from a single log. While working as a broadcaster for CBC Radio in the 1950s, Reid took a course in jewellery making at Ryerson Polytechnical Institute (now Ryerson University) in Toronto. From there he studied European jewellery making and combined those techniques with the traditions of Haida art, creating jewellery which reflected Haida society. As Reid grew famous as an artist, he became an outspoken advocate and activist for the Haida. When he died of Parkinson's disease in 1998, the Haida took his body to his mother's ancestral home in the Queen Charlotte Islands aboard *Lootaas*, his celebrated canoe sculpture. In his life, he created several hundreds of pieces of work, all of which reflect his passion and commitment to the Haida. (JAMES OSTIME)

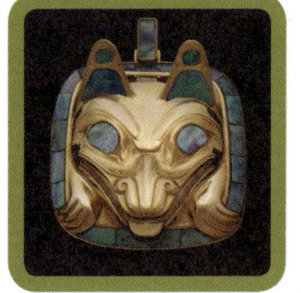

Wolf pendant.

NOVEMBER

15 **1801.** Alexander Henry recorded the Métis invention of the Red River Cart in his diary.

16 **1885.** Louis Riel was hanged for high treason at Regina, North-West Territories.

17 **1945.** Carol Geddes, Inland Tlingit filmmaker and writer, was born in Teslin, Yukon.

18

19 **1998.** *Antigone* (Cree adaptation of Sophocles' classic) by Deanne Kasokeo, Cree, and put on by the Red Tattoo Ensemble, opened at the Globe Theatre, Regina, Saskatchewan.

20 **1981.** Alberta Premier Peter Lougheed released the terms of the Alberta-Métis Association of Alberta Accord to the public. The accord reinserted federal recognition of pre-existing and existing Aboriginal rights into the draft Constitution; the accord was accepted by the House of Commons in December.

21

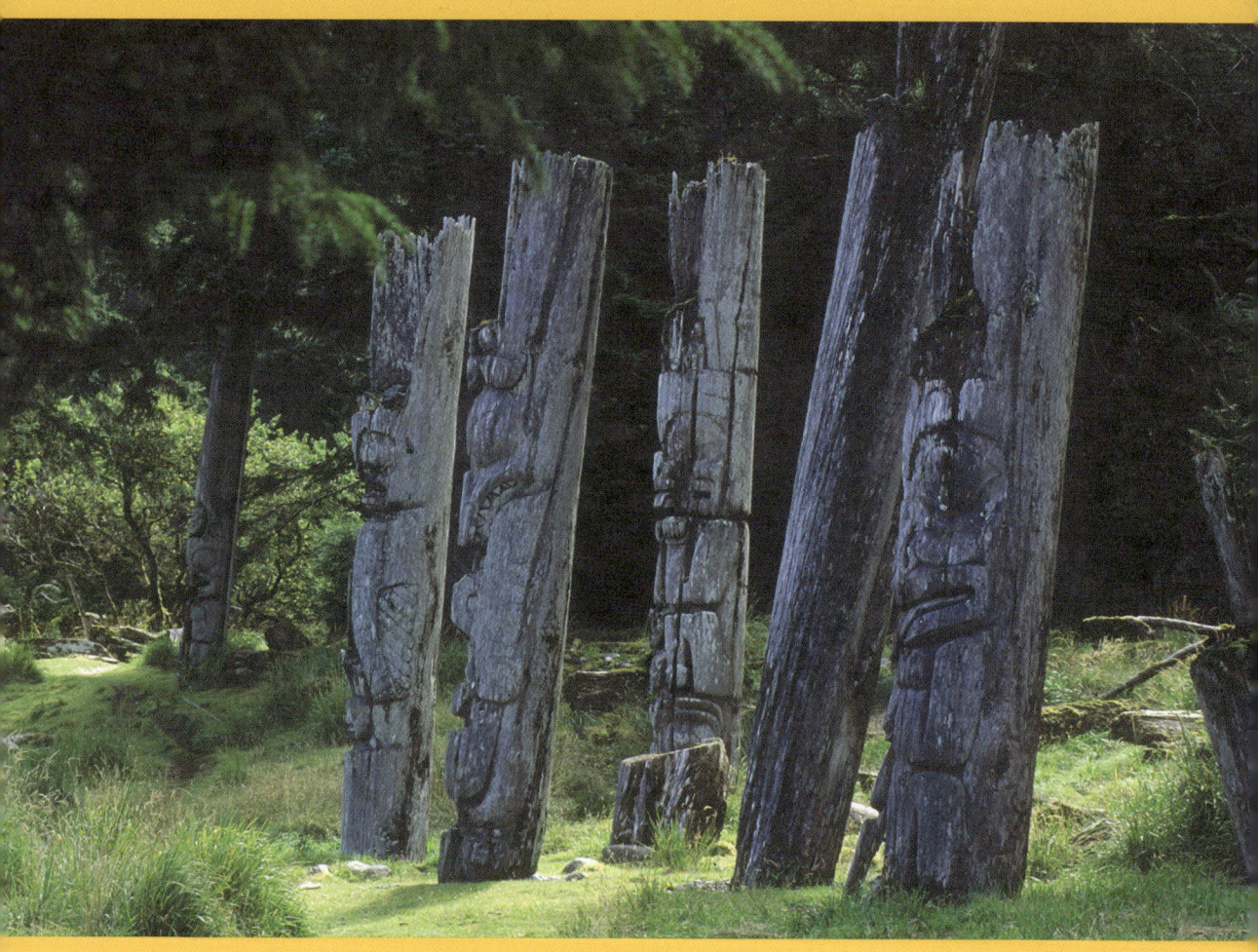

Ninstints.
This former Haida village is one of five World Heritage Sites in British Columbia.

NOVEMBER

22   **1752.** The Mi'kmaq and the British Crown signed treaties of peace and friendship in Halifax, Nova Scotia.

1957. Mohawk Olympic gold medalist Alwyn Morris was born.

23   **2005.** The Government of Canada announced a $2 billion compensation package for the approximately 86,000 survivors of Indian Residential Schools. The payout for survivors is $10,000 plus $3,000 per year attended.

24   **1807.** Joseph Brant (Thayendanegea), Mohawk military and political leader, died.

25

26

27   **1885.** Miserable Man, Bad Arrow, Round the Sky, Wandering Spirit, Iron Body, and Little Bear (Crees), and Itka and Man Without Blood (Assiniboines), were hanged at Battleford, North-West Territories, for their role in the North-West Resistance.

28

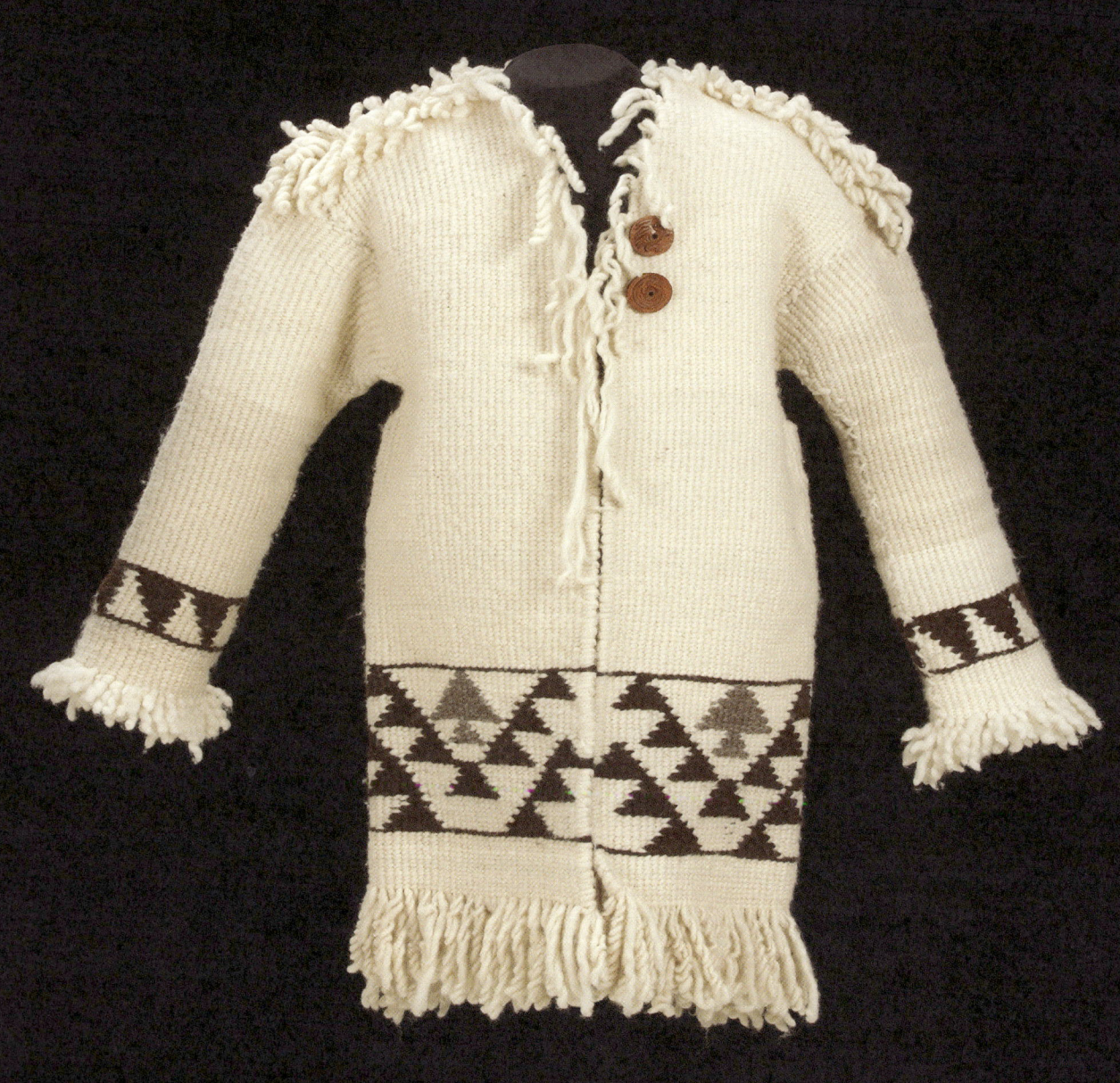

Robyn Sparrow, blanket coat.
Hand spun sheep's wool, natural dyes, wood, 1985. The design of this coat is based on a traditional Salish coat documented in early photographs. Sparrow, from the Musqueam Reserve in Vancouver, British Columbia, was at the forefront of the revival of Coast Salish loom weaving. The buttons, in the shape of miniature spindle whorls, were carved by Jim Kew, also from Musqueam.

NOVEMBER

29   **1949.** John McLeod, Mississauga writer, was born in Oakville, Ontario.

30   **1997.** The closing performance of *The Baby Blues*, by Drew Hayden Taylor, Ojibwe, was held in Toronto, Ontario.

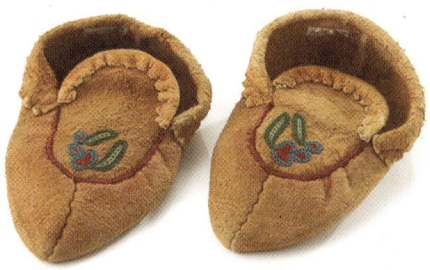

Ojibwe children's moccasins, n.d.

"I was only a housewife with a dream to bring laughter to the sad eyes of my people."

—RITA JOE, MI'KMAW POET

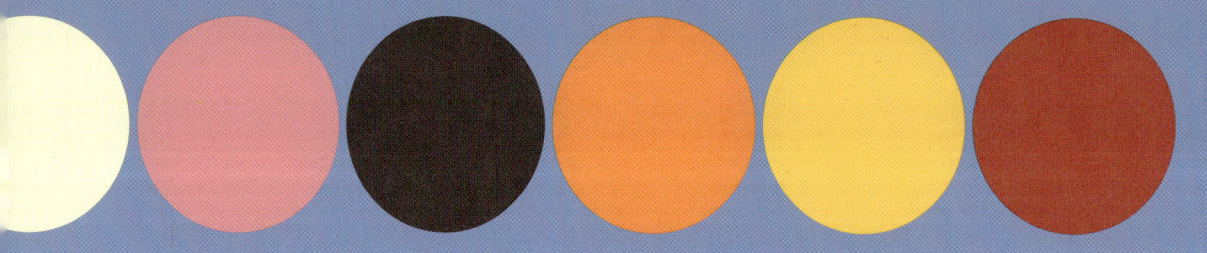

- **1643:** The "Huron Carol" ("Twas in the Moon of Wintertime") was written by Jean de Brébeuf, a Jesuit missionary.

- **1837:** Gabriel Dumont was born in St. Boniface, Red River Settlement (in present-day Winnipeg, Manitoba).

- **1987:** The Government of Alberta and the Métis Association of Alberta (now the Métis Nation of Alberta) concluded a partnership to address "Métis needs and aspirations."

december
shanáx dís
(TLINGIT)
"Unborn Seals are Getting Hair"

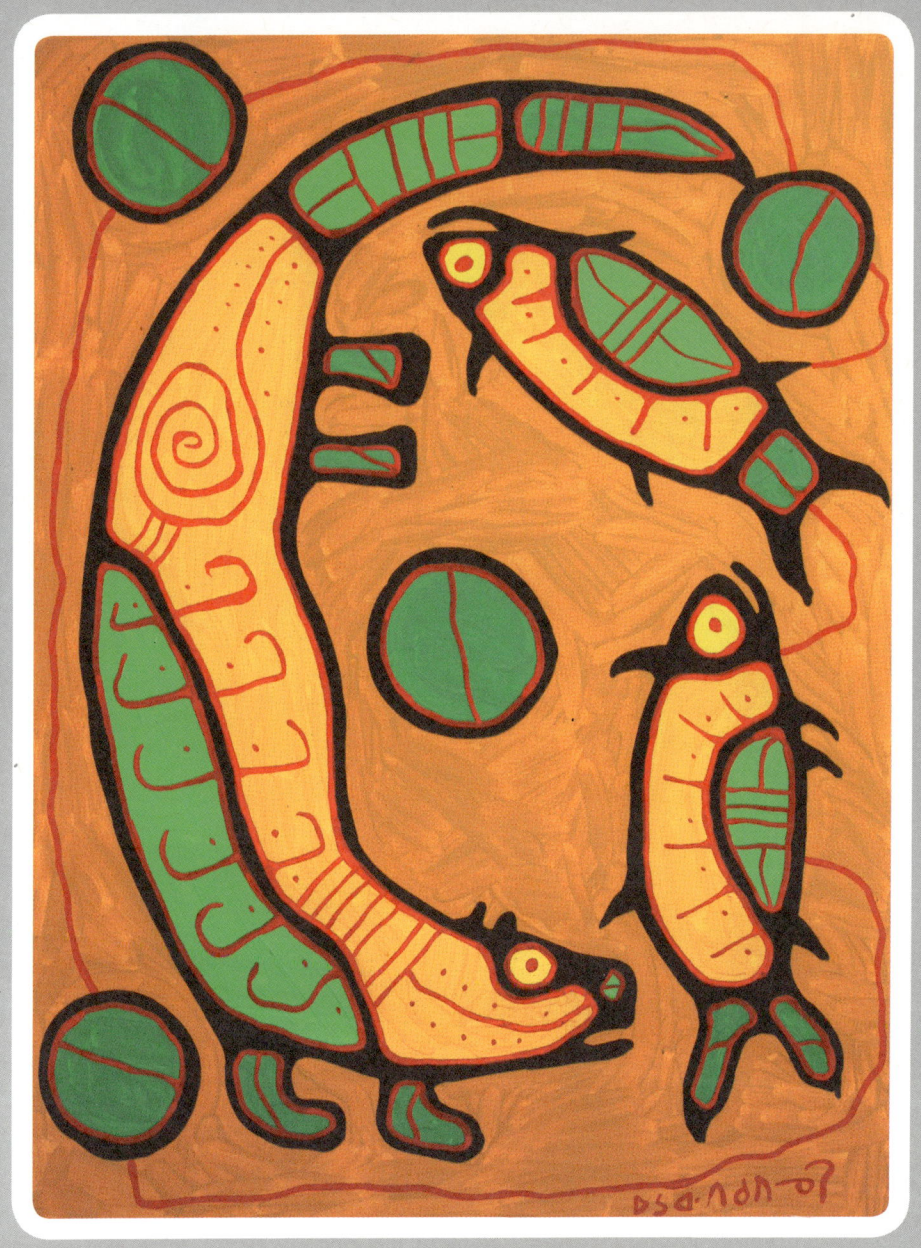

Norval Morrisseau, *Woodland Otter and Fish*.
Acrylic on canvas, 36 x 48 inches, 1992.
See March 14 and December 4.

DECEMBER

1   **2005.** The Nunatsiavut government began as a regional ethnic government for Labrador Inuit.

2

3   **1993.** *Alberta Sweetgrass,* an Aboriginal newspaper, was launched.

4   **1896.** Plains Cree Chief Ahtahkakoop (Starblanket) died at the reserve named after him.   **2007.** Artist Norval Morrisseau, a member of the "Indian Group of Seven," died.

5

6   **1951.** Tomson Highway, Cree playwright and novelist, was born on his father's trap line in Manitoba.

7

The Indian Group of Seven

The Indian Group of Seven was the cheeky name given by a reporter from the *Winnipeg Free Press* to a group of First Nations and Native American artists of such diverse ancestries as Denesuline, Ojibwe, Pueblo, and Saulteaux who in the early 1970s formed the Professional National Indian Artists Incorporation. The name echoed that of the original Group of Seven, seven Canadian artists famous for their landscape paintings in the 1920s. The landscape depicted by the Indian Group of Seven showed First Nations artistic works comparable to their western contemporaries in style, but distinctly First Nations in their content. In 1973, Daphne Odjig, Alex Janvier, and Jackson Beardy held a group show at the Winnipeg Art Gallery entitled *Treaty Numbers 23, 287, 1171*, those digits being the numbers given to each artist's band when treaties were signed with the Canadian government. The exhibition was an extremely successful one and was the impetus to an important meeting. Odjig and Beardy decided to meet with Janvier, Eddy Cobiness, Norval Morrisseau, Carl Ray, and Joe Sanchez in Odjig's home. All seven were prominent First Nations artists and all were Canadian except for Sanchez, a Native American who met Odjig and her husband when he came to Canada to escape the draft. They decided individually and as a group to support both established and up-and-coming First Nations artists and to address the issues and concerns of their artistic community. They called themselves the Professional National Indian Artists Incorporation and together held several art shows across the country. The last one in which all seven artists participated was held at Montreal's Dominion Gallery in 1975. Subsequently, they held individual exhibitions, and some of the artists taught courses throughout the country. The Indian Group of Seven had a major effect on Canada's modern art scene: prior to their exhibitions, people thought of First Nations and Native American art as only totem poles and traditional carvings. The Indian Group of Seven produced the landscapes and portraiture similar in style to their western counterparts, yet they reflected their own respective cultures and paved the way for a new generation of First Nations and Native American artists to do the same.

(JAMES OSTIME)

DECEMBER

8 **1869.** The Métis National Committee declared itself the provisional government of the Red River Settlement.

9

10 **1998.** Jim Antoine, former Chief of the Fort Simpson Dene, became premier of the Northwest Territories.

11 **1997.** The British Columbia Supreme Court ruled in *Delgamuukw* that Aboriginal title exists on an equal level with provincial Crown title and "cannot be sold, surrendered or extinguished without the consent of First Nations and can only be alienated to the Federal Crown."

12 **1934.** The Government of Alberta appointed the Ewing Commission to investigate Métis living conditions in Alberta.

13

14 **1955.** Gwen O'Soup, of the Key Indian Reserve near Kamsack, Saskatchewan, became the first woman to be elected Chief in Canada.

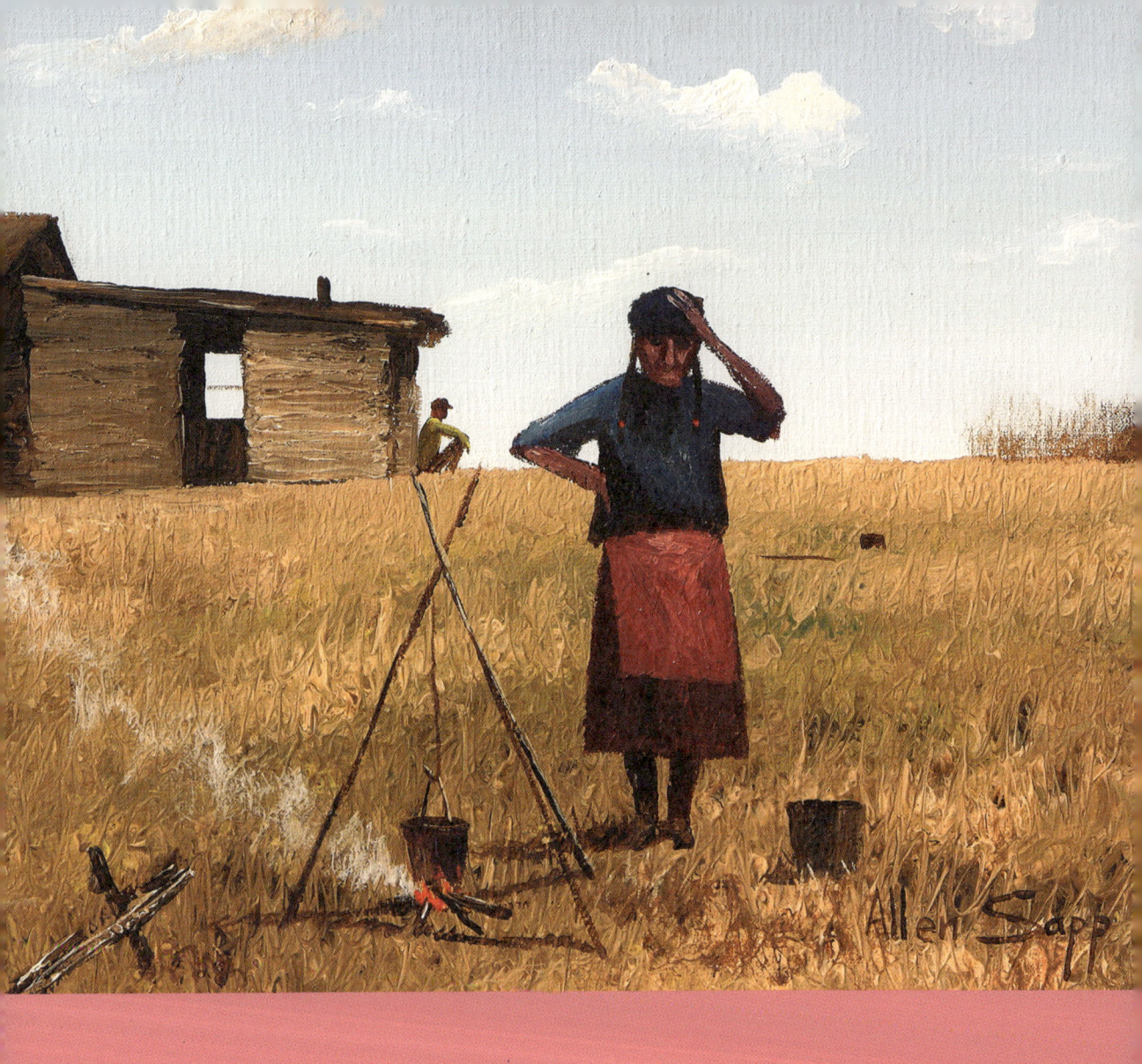

Allen Sapp, *Waiting for Water to Boil.*
Acrylic on canvas, 16 x 20 inches, 1975.
See January 2.

DECEMBER

15 **2008.** Statistics Canada reported that the average age of Aboriginals was younger than non-Aboriginals.

16 **1981.** The Government of Canada set aside $4 billion and land to settle Aboriginal claims in the Yukon and Northwest Territories.

17

18 **1968.** Mohawk from Akwasasne Reserve blocked a bridge running from their reservation and between the U.S. and Canada in order to reassert legal authority over land and to protest customs duties on their goods.

19 **1995.** Halifax, Nova Scotia, District School Board passed the Aboriginal, Black, and Visible Ethnocultural Anti-Racism Policy; the Policy was the first anti-racism policy passed by a school district in Nova Scotia.

20 **2006.** The Nunavut Court of Justice approved the Indian Residential Schools Settlement Agreement.

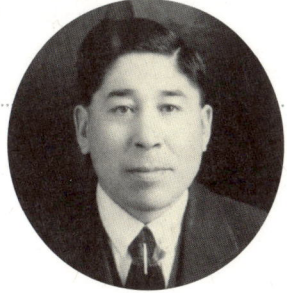

21 **1960.** Joseph Frances Dion, Cree political organizer and educator, died at Bonnyville, Alberta. He is pictured here in 1935 when he served on the Executive Committee of the Alberta Métis Association. ▲

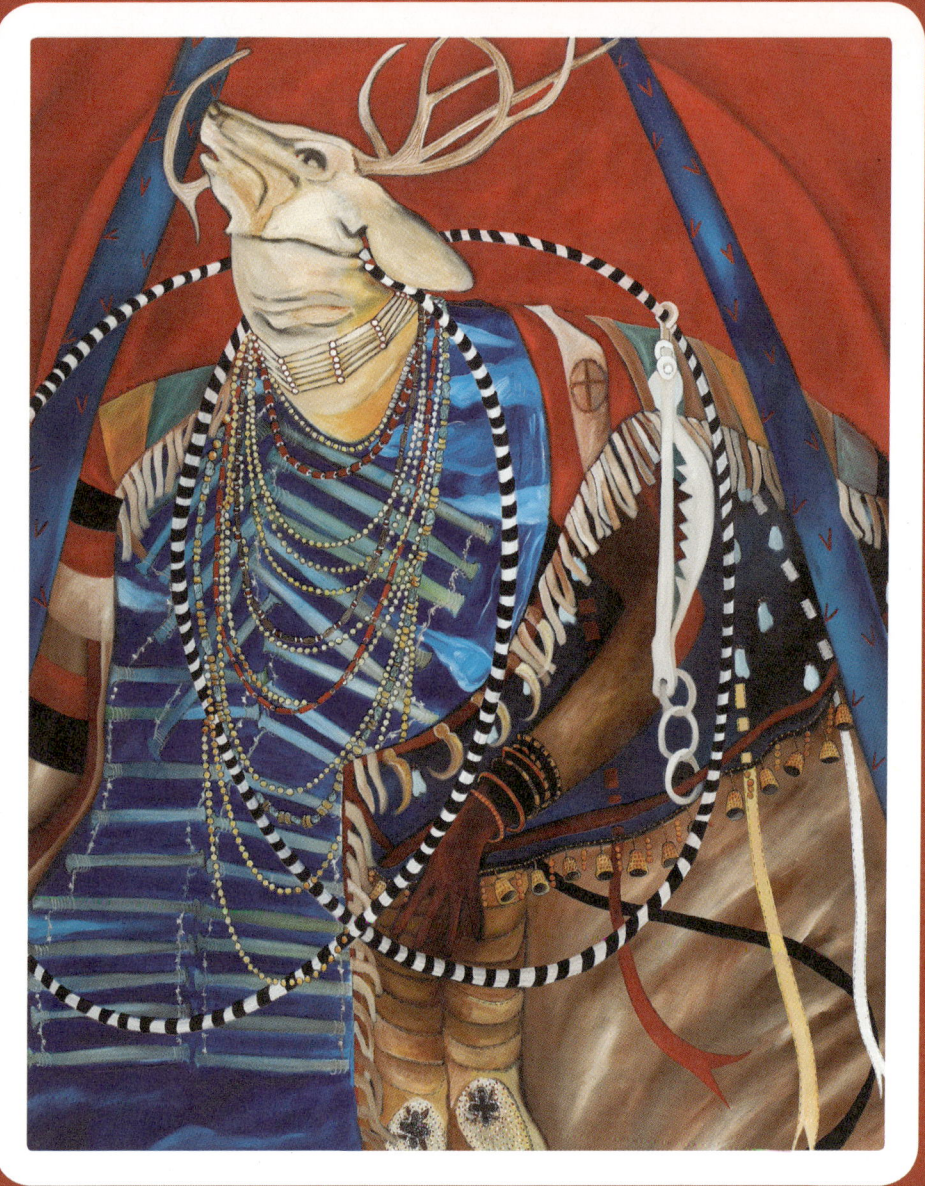

Joane Cardinal-Schubert (1942-2009), *Song of My Dream Bed Dance.*
Acrylic on canvas, 152 x 122 centimetres, 1995.

DECEMBER

22 **1967.** Gilbert C. Monture (1896-1973) was made an Officer of the Order of Canada for contributions in the public service, including many missions abroad for the United Nations. A Mohawk, Monture was a great-grandson of Joseph Brant. A member of Canada's Indian Hall of Fame, he was made an honourary chief of the Six Nations Reserve in 1958. ▼

23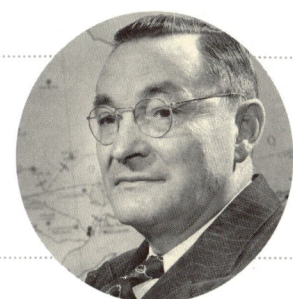

24 **1930.** Johnny Charlie was born in Rampart House, Yukon Territory. He went on to become chief of Tetlit Gwichin and, when in office, negotiated his band's land claim.

25 **1887.** Ghandl, Haida poet, was baptized as Walter McGregor by Methodist missionaries.

26

27 **1869.** Louis Riel became President of the provisional government of Rupert's Land at the Red River Settlement.

28

First Nations Actors and Actresses

Asked to name a famous First Nations actor of the past 50 years, many might think of Jay Silverheels, a Mohawk best known for his role as Tonto in the 1950s TV series, "The Lone Ranger." Like many of his First Nations contemporaries, he was often cast as an extra in "cowboys and Indians" Westerns; however, he did achieve fame and recognition as Tonto. Despite the acclaim, Silverheels had to fight the cultural misconceptions inherent in his role as the sidekick who only grunted monosyllabic replies from beneath his headdress. Since then, however, many First Nations actors and actresses have fought against "Indian" stereotypes as they portray characters as rich and varied as the cultures they come from. George Clutesi and Tom Jackson, who have appeared in several television and film roles, have an equally prolific output of novels (Clutesi) and music (Jackson) in addition to being activists for First Nations causes. Performers Michael Greyeyes and Tina Keeper have found success beyond their careers as actors: Greyeyes teaches movement at York University, and Keeper served as a member of Parliament. Some actors and actresses have achieved great acclaim: Tantoo Cardinal received several awards and nominations for her work in *Dances with Wolves* and *Legends of the Fall*; Chief Dan George was nominated for an Academy Award for his role in *Little Big Man*. Graham Greene and Gordon Tootoosis crafted careers based on their portrayals of First Nations people; however, there are performers today for whom cultural background is incidental. Tahmoh Penikett of the White River First Nation

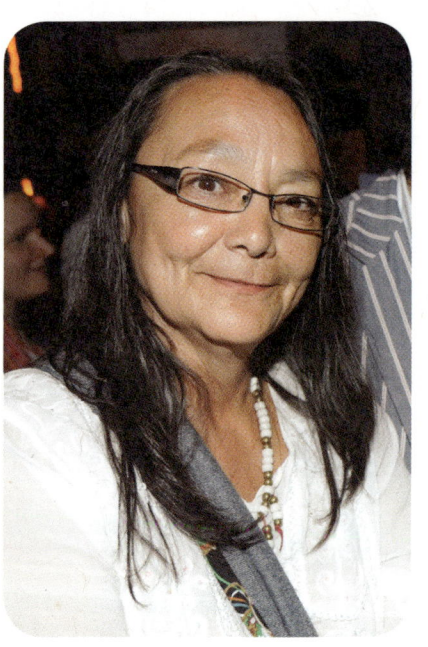

Tantoo Cardinal

DECEMBER

29

30

31   **1986.** Bronson Pelletier, Plains Cree/Métis actor, was born. Pelletier is best known for his role as "Jared" in the *Twilight* saga movies. ▶

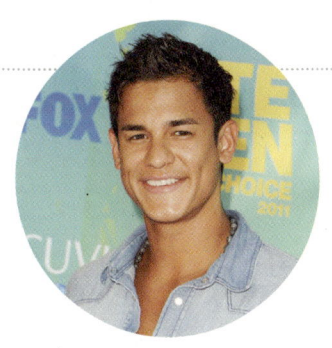

appeared on the show *Battlestar Galactica*, and Adam Beach of the Saulteaux First Nation played a detective on *Law & Order: Special Victims Unit*—in both cases cultural background had no bearing on the characters played. Cree Summer, who was on "A Different World," now does voice-overs for characters of various ages, races, and backgrounds. First Nations performers are now becoming stars with acclaim and recognition comparable to their non-First Nations counterparts. For example, Bronson Pelletier has become a celebrity worldwide for his role in the popular *Twilight* series. (JAMES OSTIME)

sky

"Sometimes I go about *pitying myself*, and all the while I am being *carried across the sky* by beautiful clouds."

—OJIBWE PROVERB

Acknowledgments

The direct and indirect contributions of a number of people have helped in the creation of this book on First Nation, Métis, and Inuit history in Canada. In reality *First in Canada* was possible only because of the wealth of resources generated by First Nation, Métis, Inuit, Indigenous peoples, and allies over millennia. I would like to thank Brian Mlazgar, Publications Manager at the University of Regina's Canadian Plains Research Center Press, for the initial offer to revise and update a calendar on First Nation and Métis history for publication in 2011 and his enthusiasm for its conversion into a book-length resource. Brian provided generous financial support and the office manager, Lorraine Nelson, assisted with administrative work that accompanied the research for the book.

Colleagues from within and outside of the University of Saskatchewan assisted with the research for the book. Sarah Nickel and Allyson Stevenson shared visual and primary sources. Bev Worsley, area director of Eastern Region III of the Métis Nation of Saskatchewan, circulated my initial request for oral, visual, and textual resources for the book. Kevin Burton at Atlantic Canada's First Nation Help Desk & *Mi'kmaw Kina'matnewey* supplied references and valuable resources for the book and assisted with the authorization of material supplied in the book

Colleagues provided valuable resources to investigate for *First in Canada*. Dates in the illustrated year relevant to the history of the Mi'kmaq and Maliseet were drawn heavily from resources at the Mi'kmaq Resource Centre at Cape Breton University, and most helpful was the "Book of Days for the Mi'kmaq Year"—a resource that is available at http://mrc.cbu.ca/calendar.html. Diane Chisholm was one of many individuals at institutions around Canada who took an interest in the book project and provided important sources that made *First in Canada* possible. I thank her especially for supplying me with a copy of the fourth edition of the *Mi'kmaw Resource Guide* that has not only valuable timelines but also reproductions of the treaties signed between the Mi'kmaq and representatives of the British Crown and the United States of America: the 1725 Treaty, the 1749 Treaty, the 1752

Treaty, the 1760 Treaty, the Treaties of 1760-1761, and Treaty of Watertown (1776). Ken Dahl of the Saskatchewan Archives Board led me to a very helpful resource entitled "Our Legacy." I also thank Dr. Jennifer S. H. Brown, Anne Lindsay, and Weldon Hiebert at the Centre for Rupert's Land Studies at the University of Winnipeg, Melanie McKinnon at Public Works and Government Services Canada, Dana Parisien at Saskatchewan Education, Graham Guest at the Northern Saskatchewan Archives, Darren Préfontaine at Gabriel Dumont Institute, Sharon Foley at the Provincial Archives of Manitoba, and Cheryl Avery at the University of Saskatchewan Archives.

The title for the book is the outcome of a discussion with Kevin Daniels, former Vice-Chief of the Congress of Aboriginal Peoples, who suggested the use of the term "Aboriginal."

Finally, I express warm gratitude to James Ostime for his contributions and support throughout this endeavour.

Thank you to everyone for your assistance with the book! All errors and omissions are my responsibility alone, and I apologize if anyone's name has been missed.

Jonathan Anuik

Image Credits

JANUARY

JAN. 1-7, FACING PAGE: Dorset Fine Arts. **JAN. 2:** Anna Willey. **JAN. 4:** Brian Bukowski, General Synod Communications, Anglican Church of Canada. **JAN. 8:** Library and Archives Canada (C-092599, watercolour on ivory, 7.7 x 6.5 cm, by Lady Henrietta Martha Hamilton, wife of the governor of Newfoundland, Sir Charles Hamilton). **JAN. 15-21, FACING PAGE:** David Neel. **JAN. 19:** Richard S. Finnie / Library and Archives Canada (e002394377). **JAN. 22-28, FACING PAGE:** Glenbow Museum (P0007732). **JAN. 27:** Glenbow Museum (NA-2864-27196). **JAN. 29-31, FACING PAGE:** Saskatchewan Archives Board (left, R-A8223-1; right, R-A8223-2).

FEBRUARY

FEB. 1-7, FACING PAGE: Library and Archives Canada (PA-007439). **FEB. 2:** www.aptn.ca. **FEB. 8-14, FACING PAGE:** Archives of Manitoba (N5732). **FEB. 10:** Archives of Manitoba (N5396). **FEB. 13:** David McLennan. **FEB. 20:** Bill Borgwardt. **FEB. 22-28/29, FACING PAGE:** Robert Davidson.

MARCH

MAR. 1-7, FACING PAGE & MAR. 7: Don Hall, Photography Department, University of Regina. **MAR. 8-14, FACING PAGE:** Library and Archives Canada (C-085125). **MAR. 12:** Don Hall, Photography Department, University of Regina. **MAR. 15-21:** Glenbow Museum (P0006685). **MAR. 22-28, FACING PAGE:** Jane Ash Poitras/Clint Buehler. **MAR. 26:** Glenbow Museum (NA-1406-212, from *Harper's Weekly*, May 9, 1885).

APRIL

APR. 1-7, FACING PAGE: Glenbow Museum (top, P0006818; bottom, P0006806). **APR. 2:** RCMP Heritage Centre (Geraldine Moodie photograph, 941.9.52). **APR. 5:** Library and Archives Canada (PA-215156). **APR. 8-14, FACING PAGE:** Jane Ash Poitras/Clint Buehler (Curtis Trent photograph). **APR. 15-21, FACING PAGE:** Catriona Jeffries Gallery. **APR. 20:** Library and Archives Canada (C-073700, *Pontiac Meeting Governor Haldimand*, watercolour with monochrome black wash over pencil, with opaque white on brown commercial board, by Charles William Jefferys, 1869-1951). **APR. 22-28:** Provincial Archives of Alberta (P129). **APR. 29-30, FACING PAGE:** left, Library and Archives Canada (C-014090); middle and right, Saskatchewan Sports Hall of Fame and Museum.

MAY

MAY 1-7, FACING PAGE: Bill Borgwardt.
MAY 2: Library and Archives Canada (PA-102697). **MAY 7:** Aboriginal Affairs and Northern Development Canada. **MAY 8-14, FACING PAGE:** Archives of Manitoba (N5781). **MAY 9:** Glenbow Museum (NA-1480-40, sketch from the *Canadian Pictorial and Illustrated War News*, August 29, 1885). **MAY 15-21, FACING PAGE:** Janvier Gallery. **MAY 20:** Getty Images. **MAY 22-28, FACING PAGE:** Saskatchewan Archives Board (R-B8775). **MAY 25:** Library and Archives Canada (PA-114838). **MAY 29-31, FACING PAGE:** Saskatchewan Archives Board (R-B4512).

JUNE

JUNE 1-7, FACING PAGE: Bill Borgwardt.
JUNE 4: Michael Greyeyes. **JUNE 8:** George Hunter Photography. **JUNE 12:** School of Journalism, University of Regina. **JUNE 15-21, FACING PAGE:** Don Hall, Photography Department, University of Regina. **JUNE 16:** Library and Archives Canada (C-073715, *The Fight at Seven Oaks, 1816*, watercolour over pencil on commercial board, by Charles William Jefferys, 1869-1951). **JUNE 22-28, FACING PAGE:** Tourism Saskatoon. **JUNE 22:** V. Tony Hauser. **JUNE 27:** Tourism Saskatoon. **JUNE 29-30, FACING PAGE:** Glenbow Museum (P0006433).

JULY

JULY 1-7, FACING PAGE: Glenbow Museum (NA-1270-1). **JULY 6:** Library and Archives Canada (e002505690). **JULY 8-14, FACING PAGE:** Saskatchewan Archives Board (R-A6277). **JULY 15-21, FACING PAGE:** Roy Antal/*Regina Leader-Post* (copyright 2001, used with permission). **JULY 20:** Getty Images. **JULY 21:** Saskatchewan Archives Board (R-A4814). **JULY 22-28, FACING PAGE:** Glenbow Museum (P0007174). **JULY 29-31, FACING PAGE:** Shaney Komulainen/ Canadian Press.

AUGUST

AUG. 8-14, FACING PAGE: Dorset Fine Arts.
AUG. 15-21, FACING PAGE: George Hunter Photography. **AUG. 21:** Library and Archives Canada (Status of Women Canada/e002415954). **AUG. 22-28, FACING PAGE:** Glenbow Museum (P0006822).
AUG. 29-31, FACING PAGE: Library and Archives Canada (PA-215127, courtesy of the Estate of Sam Tata).

SEPTEMBER

SEPT. 1-7, FACING PAGE: Glenbow Museum (NA-5178-1). **SEPT. 8-14, FACING PAGE:** Odjig Arts. **SEPT. 10:** David McLennan. **SEPT. 15-21, FACING PAGE:** Library and Archives Canada (C-003863). **SEPT. 25:** Heather Simeney MacLeod. **SEPT. 29-30, FACING PAGE:** National Gallery of Canada/Estate of Carl Beam.

OCTOBER

OCT. 1-7, FACING PAGE: Library and Archives Canada (C-40894). **OCT. 8-14, FACING PAGE:** Gordon F. Sedawie, Vancouver Public Library, Special Collections (VPL 44651, with permission of Pacific Press). **OCT. 15-21, FACING PAGE:** Martin Lipman. **OCT. 15:** Glenbow Museum (NA-4216-14). **OCT. 22-28, FACING PAGE:** National Speakers Bureau (http://nsb.com/speakers/view/tomson-highway). **OCT. 29-31, FACING PAGE:** Glenbow Museum (P0006684).

NOVEMBER

NOV. 1-7, FACING PAGE: Bill Reid Foundation (Collection No. 36, courtesy of the Bill Reid Estate, photograph by Kenji Nagai). **NOV. 8-14:** Doris Rowe. **NOV. 22-28, FACING PAGE:** Duane Sept Photography. **NOV. 29-30, FACING PAGE:** Glenbow Museum (P0006682). **NOV. 29-30:** Glenbow Museum (P0007303).

DECEMBER

DEC. 1-7, FACING PAGE: Coghlan Art Studio and Gallery (Copyright Gabe Vadas, all rights reserved, Estate of Norval Morrisseau). **DEC. 15-21, FACING PAGE:** Permanent Collection of the Allen Sapp Gallery. **DEC. 21:** Glenbow Museum (PA-2218-109). **DEC. 22-28, FACING PAGE:** National Gallery of Canada (Courtesy of the Estate of Joane Cardinal-Schubert: Mike Schubert, Christopher Schubert, and Justin Schubert). **DEC. 22:** George Hunter Photography. **DEC. 29-31:** Getty Images. **DEC. 31:** Getty Images.